MONEY SKILLS FOR THE ANXIOUS GENERATION

Empowering Millennials and Gen Z to Take Control of Their Finances and Build a Secure Future

MADISON BLAIR

Copyright © 2024 by Madison Blair

All rights reserved. No part of this book may be reproduced or transmitted in any form or by any means, electronic or mechanical, including photocopying, recording, or by any information storage and retrieval system, without permission in writing from the publisher.

The information provided in this book is designed to provide helpful information on the subjects discussed. The author and publisher disclaim any liability or loss in connection with the use or misuse of this information. It is recommended that readers consult with appropriate professionals before taking any actions based on the information in this book.

DEDICATION

This book is for you – the ones who refuse to settle, who dare to imagine a brighter financial future, and who have the guts to chase it.

WHY THIS BOOK?

Because money shouldn't be a mystery. Because financial freedom isn't just for the lucky few. Because you deserve to live a life unburdened by money worries, free to pursue your passions and create the life you've always dreamed of.

I wrote this for every late-night worrier, every paycheck-to-paycheck survivor, and every aspiring entrepreneur with a fire in their belly. I wrote it for those who've been told "that's just how it is" one too many times.

This book is a rebellion against financial fear, a toolkit for turning dreams into dollars, and a roadmap to the life you deserve.

TABLE OF CONTENTS

Dedication 3

Why this book? 4

CHAPTER 1 15

   THE MONEY TRAP 15

      Understanding Our Generation's Financial Fears. 16

      Breaking the Chains 19

CHAPTER 2 25

   MIND OVER MONEY 25

      The Psychology of Spending: Why We Buy What We Don't Need 26

      Techniques to Overcome Financial Anxiety 32

CHAPTER 3 39

   BUDGETING WITHOUT THE BULLSH*T 39

      The Anti-Budget: A Fresh Approach to Managing Your Cash 40

      Tracking Like a Pro 47

CHAPTER 4 55

SLAYING THE STUDENT LOAN DRAGON (AND OTHER BEASTS) 55

    The Loan Ranger 56

    Debt Snowball vs. Avalanche 64

CHAPTER 5 73

    THE EMERGENCY FUND 73

    From Zero to Hero: Building Your First $1,000 Safety Net 74

    Leveling Up: Strategies for a Fully-Funded Emergency Account 78

CHAPTER 6 85

    INVESTING FOR THE CLUELESS 85

    Demystifying the Stock Market 86

    Beyond Stocks: Exploring Real Estate, Bonds, and More 92

CHAPTER 7 99

    THE SIDE HUSTLE REVOLUTION 99

    Finding Your Niche 100

    From Hobby to Empire: Scaling Your Side Hustle 106

CHAPTER 8 113

   CRYPTO DECODED 113

      Understanding Cryptocurrency Basics 114

      To HODL or Not to HODL: Smart Strategies for Crypto Investing... 123

CHAPTER 9 131

   THE RETIREMENT RIDDLE.. 131

      401(k)s, IRAs, and WTFs 132

      The Fire Movement: Is Early Retirement Possible? 140

CHAPTER 10 149

   LIVING RICH 149

      The Art of Mindful Spending 150

      Aligning Your Finances with Your Values 155

Thank you from the bottom of my heart for choosing this book. Your support means the world to me, and I truly appreciate your investment in these ideas. It's my hope that the insights shared here will inspire and empower you on your journey. Wishing you all the success and fulfillment as you take steps toward living the life you envision.

INTRODUCTION

"Money doesn't buy happiness, but it sure as hell pays for peace of mind."

I scribbled those words in my notebook during my first year as a financial advisor. Little did I know then how often I'd return to that simple truth in my work with Millennials and Gen Z over the past decade.

Hey there. I'm Madison Blair, and I've spent the last ten years in the trenches of personal finance, helping young adults get their money shit together. And let me tell you, it's been one hell of a ride.

When I started out, fresh-faced and armed with a finance degree, I thought I had all the answers. Boy, was I wrong. The textbooks hadn't prepared me for the real-world money struggles of my peers – the crushing student debt, the gig economy hustle, the FOMO-fueled spending sprees, and the paralyzing anxiety that comes with it all.

I've sat across from 23-year-olds with six-figure student loans and no idea how to start paying them off. I've coached 30-somethings still living paycheck to paycheck, dreaming of homeownership but seeing it slip further away each year. I've consoled countless young adults who feel like they're drowning in a sea of financial obligations, with no life raft in sight.

Nevertheless, I've also witnessed incredible transformations. I've seen people go from financial disaster to debt-free in 18 months. I've watched as anxiety turned into confidence, and money fears morphed into excitement about the future. And I'm here to tell you: if they can do it, so can you.

This book isn't some magic bullet or get-rich-quick scheme. If that's what you're after, you can stop reading now and go buy a lottery ticket instead. What you'll find in these pages is real talk about money – the kind of honest, sometimes uncomfortable conversations I have with my clients every day.

We're going to dig into the nitty-gritty of why so many of us are stressed about money. Spoiler alert: it's not just because we're buying too many lattes (though we'll talk about that too). We'll look at the perfect storm of economic factors, societal pressures, and yes, some of our own habits that have led to what I call the "Anxious Generation."

Did you know that 76% of Millennials and 68% of Gen Z report that money is a significant source of stress in their lives? Or that the average student loan debt for the Class of 2023 was a whopping $37,574? These aren't just cold statistics – they're the lived reality of millions of young adults trying to build a life in an economy that often feels rigged against them.

But here's the good news: it doesn't have to be this way. You don't have to lie awake at night worrying about your credit card balance or feel a pit in your stomach every time you check your bank account. Financial peace of mind isn't just for the rich or the lucky – it's achievable for anyone willing to learn and put in the work.

Throughout this book, we'll cover everything from rewiring your money mindset to practical strategies for budgeting, investing, and building wealth. We'll talk about how to tackle debt without losing your sanity, how to build an emergency fund that actually makes you feel secure, and yes, even how to invest in crypto without feeling like you're gambling your future away.

But this isn't just about numbers on a spreadsheet. Money touches every aspect of our lives – our relationships, our career choices, our mental health. So we'll also dive into the emotional side of finance. How do you balance saving for the future with living in the present? How do you align your spending with your values? How do you talk about money with your partner without wanting to tear your hair out?

I promise you this: by the time you finish this book, you'll have a clearer understanding of your finances and a concrete plan to improve them. You'll have tools to manage financial stress and anxiety. And most importantly, you'll have hope – because financial freedom isn't some far-off dream. It's within your reach, starting right now.

Look, I know money talk can be boring as hell. I've seen enough glazed-over eyes in my workshops to know that. So I've done my best to keep things real, relatable, and occasionally even funny (financial humor is tough, but I try). You'll find stories from real people – some of my clients, some of my friends, and yes, even some of my own money fails – sprinkled throughout these pages.

Here's what you won't find: judgment. I'm not here to lecture you about your spending habits or make you feel guilty about your debt. We've all made money mistakes (trust me, I've made my share), and shame never helped anyone's bank account grow. What you will find is honesty, empathy, and a whole lot of practical advice.

So, who is this book for? It's for the recent grad staring down the barrel of student loan repayments. It's for the young professional trying to figure out if they can afford to move out of their parents' house. It's for the side-hustler dreaming of turning their passion project into a full-time gig. It's for anyone who's ever felt overwhelmed, anxious, or just plain confused about money.

In other words, it's for you.

I won't promise that this book will make you a millionaire overnight. But I will promise that if you commit to the principles and practices in these pages, you'll end up with more money in your pocket, more confidence in your financial decisions, and yes, more of that elusive peace of mind.

So, are you ready to take control of your financial future? To stop letting money anxiety run your life? To build the kind of wealth that gives you options and freedom?

Then let's dive in. We've got work to do, and your future self is counting on you. Trust me, they'll thank you for picking up this book.

Welcome to "Money Skills for The Anxious Generation." Let's get started on building that secure future you deserve.

CHAPTER 1

THE MONEY TRAP

UNDERSTANDING OUR GENERATION'S FINANCIAL FEARS

"More than 60% of Millennials feel anxious when they think about their finances, and for Gen Z, it's not much better." This stat might surprise you, but it's the reality we're living in. As someone who's spent years working with young adults, I've seen firsthand the sleepless nights, the constant worry, and the overwhelming sense of dread that money—or the lack of it—can cause.

Let's start by talking about the elephant in the room: debt. Whether it's student loans, credit card debt, or medical bills, Millennials and Gen Z are drowning in it. Take Bronwyn, a 29-year-old marketing professional. She landed her dream job right out of college, but the $45,000 in student loans she's carrying around feels like a ball and chain. Every month, she's paying off interest, but the principal amount barely seems to shrink. She confided in me that she often feels like she's running on a treadmill, going nowhere fast. The weight of this debt is enough to make anyone anxious.

But it's not just the debt that's causing sleepless nights. The job market is another beast. Sure, we've got more opportunities than ever before, thanks to the gig economy and technological advancements, but that also means less stability. I've met countless young professionals who are juggling multiple side hustles, not because they want to, but because they have to. The fear of being laid off, or worse, not being able to find a job in the first place, looms large. Even those with steady jobs aren't immune; they worry about being replaced by automation or the next wave of AI.

Let's not forget the rising cost of living. It's almost impossible to talk about financial anxiety without mentioning housing. In cities like New York or San Francisco, the idea of owning a home seems as far-fetched as winning the lottery. Renting isn't much better. I recently spoke to James, a 26-year-old software engineer, who's spending nearly half his income on a tiny apartment in a decent neighborhood. He's been putting off saving for retirement because, as he put it, "How can I think about 40 years from now when I'm just trying to make it through this month?"

There's also the pressure to keep up with the Joneses except now, the Joneses are on Instagram, flaunting their seemingly perfect lives. Social media has created this distorted reality where everyone looks like they've got it all figured out. But behind those curated posts are people just like you, struggling with the same fears and anxieties. I've had clients tell me they feel like they're failing because they can't afford the vacations, the gadgets, or the lifestyle they see online. This constant comparison is eroding their financial confidence, making them feel like they're always falling short.

Then there's the uncertainty of the future. Climate change, political instability, and economic volatility are all contributing to a general sense of unease. Young people today are acutely aware that the world is changing rapidly, and not always for the better. This uncertainty seeps into their financial decisions, making it hard to plan for the long term when the future feels so unpredictable.

Nevertheless, the anxieties you're feeling are shared by millions of others, and they're not a reflection of your worth or abilities. They're a response to real, tangible challenges that our generation is facing. Understanding these challenges is the first step in overcoming them. We can't control the economy or the job market, but we can control how we respond to these stressors.

BREAKING THE CHAINS

"Financial freedom is available to those who learn about it and work for it." – **Robert Kiyosaki**

Step 1: Acknowledge and Understand Your Financial Anxiety

The first step to breaking free from the chains of financial anxiety is to face it head-on. It's common to feel overwhelmed when thinking about money, especially when it feels like there's never enough. You're not alone in this struggle. Many young adults find themselves in a similar position, but recognizing that anxiety is the first step towards taking control.

Think about what triggers your anxiety. Is it the thought of bills piling up? The fear of not having enough saved for emergencies? Or maybe it's the pressure to keep up with peers who seem to have it all together? Whatever it is, acknowledging these feelings is crucial. They're real, but they don't have to define you.

Grab a piece of paper or open a journal and write down your financial fears. By putting them into words, you're beginning to take power away from them. Anxiety is a natural response to uncertainty. This understanding should allow you to start building a plan to tackle it.

Step 2: Start with Small Wins

Once you've acknowledged your financial anxiety, the next step is to take action, but not just any action—small, manageable steps that give you immediate wins. You don't need to tackle everything at once. In fact, trying to do so can lead to more stress. Instead, focus on something small that you can do today.

For example, start by setting up automatic transfers to a savings account, even if it's just $10 a week. That small action creates a positive momentum and shows you that you're capable of managing your finances, no matter how tight things are. Every dollar saved is a step toward breaking free from financial worry.

If you have credit card debt, commit to paying a little more than the minimum balance each month. Even an extra $20 can reduce your debt faster than you think, and more importantly, it's a win you can build on. Celebrate these small victories—they're the building blocks of your financial confidence.

Step 3: Educate Yourself without Overwhelming Yourself

Knowledge is power, but too much information at once can be paralyzing. The goal here is to build your financial literacy one step at a time. Start with the basics: budgeting, saving, and understanding interest rates.

You don't need to become a financial expert overnight. Instead, dedicate just 15 minutes a day to learning something new about personal finance. Listen to a podcast while you're on the go, read a chapter from a financial book which is what you are doing right now, or watch a YouTube video that breaks down a financial concept you've been struggling with.

The key is consistency. Over time, these small daily doses of financial education will accumulate, giving you the tools and confidence you need to make informed decisions. Remember, every expert was once a beginner. You're not expected to know everything right away, but every little bit you learn chips away at the anxiety that comes from feeling lost.

Step 4: Create a Simple Budget and Stick to It

Budgeting doesn't have to be complicated. In fact, the simpler it is, the more likely you are to stick with it. Start by tracking your income and expenses for a month. You might be surprised where your money is going. Those little purchases add up.

Once you have a clear picture of your spending habits, categorize your expenses into needs and wants. This isn't about depriving yourself, but rather understanding where you can cut back without sacrificing your happiness. Allocate a specific amount to each category and make sure your total expenses don't exceed your income.

If your budget reveals that you're spending more than you're earning, don't panic. This is just an opportunity to make adjustments. Maybe it's time to cut down on dining out or find a more affordable cell phone plan. These changes may seem small, but they add up over time.

Sticking to a budget isn't about being perfect; it's about being consistent. Give yourself grace if you slip up one month. What matters is that you get back on track and continue moving forward.

We are going to talk more on budgeting later on.

Step 5: Build an Emergency Fund

One of the greatest sources of financial anxiety is the fear of the unknown. Life is unpredictable, and unexpected expenses can throw even the most well-planned budget into disarray. This is where an emergency fund comes in.

Aim to save at least three to six months' worth of living expenses. This might sound daunting, especially if you're just starting out, but remember, you're not trying to do it all at once. Start small, with a goal of saving $500, then $1,000. Every contribution to your emergency fund, no matter how small, is a step toward financial security.

Knowing that you have a cushion to fall back on in case of emergencies can significantly reduce financial stress. It's not about being prepared for every possible scenario, but rather giving yourself peace of mind that you're protected against the unexpected.

Step 6: Surround Yourself with Support

You don't have to do this alone. Whether it's a trusted friend, family member, or financial advisor, having someone to talk to about your financial goals and challenges can make a huge difference. They can offer advice, hold you accountable, and provide the encouragement you need when things get tough.

Consider joining a community of like-minded individuals who are also working toward financial freedom. Whether it's an online forum, a local meetup, or a group of friends, being surrounded by others who understand what you're going through can be incredibly motivating.

You're not just in this for yourself—you're part of a larger movement of young adults taking control of their financial futures.

Step 7: Visualize Your Financial Freedom

Finally, take a moment to visualize what financial freedom looks like for you. Maybe it's being able to travel without worrying about money, buying your first home, or simply having peace of mind knowing that you're in control of your finances. Whatever it is, keep that vision in the forefront of your mind.

When anxiety starts to creep in, remind yourself why you're doing this. You're not just breaking free from financial anxiety—you're building a life of freedom, security, and fulfillment. Every step you take, no matter how small, is bringing you closer to that vision.

CHAPTER 2

MIND OVER MONEY

THE PSYCHOLOGY OF SPENDING: WHY WE BUY WHAT WE DON'T NEED

"We buy things we don't need with money we don't have to impress people we don't like."—**Dave Ramsey**

If you've ever found yourself standing in a checkout line, clutching something you never planned to buy, congratulations! You're officially part of the human race. We've all been there—seduced by the 50% off sign, tempted by the "last chance" banner, or lured in by the promise of free shipping. But why do we do this? What drives us to spend money on things we don't need, especially when we know deep down that it's not the best decision for our wallets?

The Social Comparison Trap

Let's start with the notorious culprit: social comparison. Picture this—you're scrolling through Instagram, and there it is. Your friend just posted a photo of their new car, the latest gadget, or that dreamy vacation in Bali. Suddenly, your perfectly functional 5-year-old car, your trusty but outdated phone, or your weekend trip to the local park feels embarrassingly inadequate. So, what do you do? You start looking for ways to upgrade your own life, not necessarily because you need it, but because you want to keep up with everyone else.

This phenomenon isn't new. Social comparison theory, first proposed by psychologist Leon Festinger in 1954, suggests that we determine our own social and personal worth based on how we stack up against others. In today's digital age, the opportunity for comparison is endless. We're constantly bombarded with images of other people's successes, purchases, and lifestyles, which can create a feeling of inadequacy or FOMO (fear of missing out). The result? A subconscious urge to spend money on things that will help us "keep up" with the perceived standard.

The Instant Gratification Monster

Now, let's talk about that little voice in your head that screams, "I want it now!"—the instant gratification monster. You know, the one that convinces you that you absolutely cannot wait another day for that new pair of shoes, even though payday is still a week away. The desire for instant gratification is a powerful force, and it's one that marketers have mastered the art of exploiting.

Our brains are wired to seek out pleasure and avoid pain, and instant gratification offers a quick hit of dopamine—

the feel-good hormone. When you buy something, especially on impulse, your brain lights up like a Christmas tree, rewarding you with a temporary high. The problem is, this high is fleeting, and once it wears off, you're left with the same old issues—plus a lighter bank account.

Emotional Spending: Retail Therapy Gone Wrong

Ever had a bad day and found yourself on Amazon, mindlessly adding items to your cart? Or maybe you've treated yourself to a fancy dinner after a stressful week, even though you're trying to save money. This is emotional spending at its finest—a way to self-soothe, distract, or reward yourself through purchases.

Emotional spending is tricky because it often happens subconsciously. You might tell yourself you deserve that expensive latte because you've worked hard, or that you need that new gadget to make life easier. While there's nothing wrong with treating yourself occasionally, emotional spending becomes a problem when it turns into a habit—a habit that drains your savings and leaves you feeling guilty afterward.

The Subscription Slippery Slope

You sign up for a free trial of a streaming service to watch that one show everyone's talking about. Before you know it, you're subscribed to five different services, each one promising exclusive content you can't live without. But here's the kicker—how often do you actually use all of them?

Subscription services are the epitome of unnecessary spending because they're often easy to overlook. It's just a few dollars a month, right? But those few dollars add up, especially when multiplied across multiple platforms. The convenience of having everything at your fingertips is alluring, but it can also lead to a bloated budget filled with charges for things you rarely use.

My Own Brush with Impulse Buying

I'm no stranger to the allure of impulse buying. I once bought a ridiculously overpriced juicer because I was convinced it would turn me into one of those health-conscious people who drink kale smoothies every morning. Spoiler alert: I used it exactly three times before it became a glorified dust collector. That's right—I paid top dollar for something that now serves as a reminder of my brief and expensive flirtation with healthy living.

I tell this story not to shame myself (okay, maybe a little), but to highlight how easy it is to get caught up in the moment. The juicer represented an ideal version of myself that I wanted to become. The reality? I don't even like kale that much.

So, how do we break free from the psychological traps that lead to unnecessary spending

Practice Mindful Spending: Before making a purchase, ask yourself why you want it and how it aligns with your long-term goals. Is it a need or a want? Will it add real value to your life, or is it just a temporary fix?

Delay Gratification: If you find something you want to buy, give yourself a cooling-off period—say 24 hours or a week. Often, the urge to buy will fade, and you'll realize you didn't need it after all.

Unsubscribe: Go through your monthly subscriptions and cancel the ones you rarely use. It's easy to lose track of these small expenses, but they can add up quickly.

Limit Social Media Time: Reduce the time you spend on social media, where you're most likely to compare yourself to others. Out of sight, out of mind.

Focus on Experiences, Not Things: Research shows that people derive more lasting happiness from experiences rather than material goods. Instead of buying the latest gadget, consider investing in experiences that create memories.

We're all susceptible to the psychology of spending—it's part of being human. But with a little self-awareness and discipline, we can make smarter financial choices that lead to a more fulfilling and financially secure life. The next time you find yourself reaching for your wallet, take a moment to reflect on why you're making that purchase. Is it truly necessary, or are you trying to fill an emotional void or keep up with others? Your bank account—and future self—will thank you for it.

TECHNIQUES TO OVERCOME FINANCIAL ANXIETY

"It's not your salary that makes you rich, it's your spending habits."—**Charles A. Jaffe**

In a world where money can often feel like both a blessing and a burden, developing a healthier relationship with your finances is essential. The anxiety that accompanies financial decisions is not uncommon, but it doesn't have to control your life. By blending mindfulness practices with practical financial strategies, you can transform the way you think about and interact with money, creating a sense of calm and clarity that will serve you in every aspect of your financial life.

Before we dive into techniques to manage financial anxiety, it's important to understand what it is and where it comes from. Financial anxiety is the fear or stress associated with money matters, whether it's worrying about paying bills, managing debt, or saving for the future. This anxiety can manifest in various ways, from sleepless nights to avoiding financial responsibilities altogether.

The root of financial anxiety often lies in our beliefs and attitudes toward money, which are shaped by our upbringing, personal experiences, and societal influences. For many, money is tied to feelings of security, self-worth, and success. When these feelings are threatened—whether by a job loss, unexpected expenses, or simply the pressure to "keep up"—anxiety can take hold.

Practicing Mindfulness in Money Matters

Mindfulness, at its core, is about being fully present and aware in the moment, without judgment. When applied to money, mindfulness encourages us to approach our finances with intention and awareness, rather than reacting impulsively or emotionally.

1. The 24-Hour Rule for Purchases

One of the simplest and most effective mindfulness techniques for managing your spending is the 24-hour rule. Whenever you feel the urge to make a non-essential purchase, pause and wait for 24 hours before making a decision. This pause allows you to reflect on whether the purchase is truly necessary or if it's driven by a temporary emotion like boredom, stress, or the desire to keep up with others.

During this 24-hour period, ask yourself:

- Why do I want this item?

- How will it add value to my life?
- Will I still want it tomorrow or next week?

More often than not, you'll find that the impulse fades, and you can make a more informed, thoughtful decision that aligns with your long-term goals.

2. Keeping a Money Journal

A money journal is another powerful tool for practicing mindfulness around your finances. This practice involves regularly recording your thoughts, feelings, and behaviors related to money. By documenting your financial experiences, you can identify patterns, triggers, and emotional responses that contribute to your financial anxiety.

- Set aside a few minutes each day or week to reflect on your financial experiences.
- Write about any purchases you made, noting the circumstances and emotions involved.
- Record any financial decisions you're facing and explore the underlying fears or concerns.
- Reflect on your financial goals and whether your actions are supporting them.

Over time, your money journal will provide valuable insights into your relationship with money, helping you to make more mindful, intentional choices.

3. Practicing Financial Meditation

Meditation is a powerful practice for calming the mind and reducing stress, and it can be especially beneficial when dealing with financial anxiety. By focusing on your breath and bringing awareness to the present moment, you can create a sense of inner peace that makes it easier to manage financial worries.

1. Find a quiet, comfortable place where you won't be disturbed.
2. Sit or lie down in a relaxed position.
3. Close your eyes and take a few deep breaths, allowing your body to relax with each exhale.
4. Bring to mind a financial concern or decision that's been causing you stress.
5. As you focus on this concern, notice any physical sensations in your body—tightness in your chest, tension in your shoulders, etc.
6. Now, shift your focus to your breath. With each inhale, imagine breathing in calm, steady energy. With each exhale, release any tension or anxiety.

7. After a few minutes, gently bring your attention back to the financial concern. Notice if your perspective has shifted or if you feel more at ease.
8. When you're ready, slowly open your eyes and return to your day.

Practicing this meditation regularly can help you approach financial decisions with a clearer, calmer mind.

4. Visualization for Financial Success

Visualization is another mindfulness technique that can be applied to money matters. By visualizing your financial goals and the steps you need to take to achieve them, you can create a positive, empowering mindset that motivates you to take action.

1. Close your eyes and take a few deep breaths to center yourself.
2. Visualize your ideal financial situation—this could be paying off debt, building savings, or achieving a specific financial milestone.
3. Imagine yourself taking the necessary steps to reach this goal. See yourself making mindful spending choices, sticking to a budget, or investing wisely.

4. As you visualize these actions, notice how you feel—confident, empowered, and in control of your finances.
5. Spend a few minutes fully immersed in this visualization, allowing the positive emotions to strengthen your resolve.
6. When you're ready, open your eyes and take a moment to reflect on the experience.

Regular visualization can help reinforce your financial goals and keep you focused on the steps needed to achieve them.

Commit to practicing this exercise and you will notice a positive change in no time.

5. Reframing Financial Setbacks

Finally, let's talk about reframing—a mindfulness technique that involves changing the way you think about a situation. Financial setbacks are inevitable, whether it's an unexpected expense, a job loss, or an investment that didn't pan out. Instead of viewing these setbacks as failures, try reframing them as opportunities for growth and learning.

For example, if you find yourself overwhelmed by debt, instead of thinking, "I'm never going to get out of this," reframe it to, "This is an opportunity to learn more about managing my finances and building a stronger foundation for the future." This shift in perspective can reduce anxiety and empower you to take positive steps forward.

I want you to know that you have the power to change your financial narrative, one mindful moment at a time.

CHAPTER 3

BUDGETING WITHOUT THE BULLSH*T

THE ANTI-BUDGET: A FRESH APPROACH TO MANAGING YOUR CASH

"Budgets are like New Year's resolutions for your wallet – everyone makes them, nobody sticks to them."

I overheard that gem at a coffee shop last week, and I couldn't help but laugh. Because let's face it, it's painfully true. We've all been there, haven't we? Sitting down with a spreadsheet, full of determination, vowing that this time we'll stick to our budget. This time we'll track every penny. This time we'll transform into the paragon of financial responsibility.

And then life happens.

You know how it goes. Your favorite band announces a surprise concert. Your car decides it's the perfect time for an expensive meltdown. Or maybe you just had a crappy day at work and that new pair of shoes is calling your name louder than Morgan Freeman narrating a nature documentary.

Suddenly, that meticulously crafted budget is about as useful as a chocolate teapot.

According to a study by U.S. Bank, only 41% of Americans use a budget. And I'd bet my last dollar that a good chunk of that 41% are lying to themselves about how well they stick to it.

So, why do traditional budgets fail so spectacularly? Well, pull up a chair and grab a coffee (or a beer, I won't judge), because we're about to dive into the anti-budget: a fresh approach to managing your cash that doesn't make you want to pull your hair out.

First things first: traditional budgets are the financial equivalent of a crash diet. They're restrictive, unsustainable, and usually leave you feeling deprived and miserable. They're all about denial – don't buy this, cut back on that, live on ramen noodles and tap water. It's like trying to lose weight by eating nothing but kale. Sure, it might work for a week or two, but eventually, you're going to crack and devour an entire pizza in one sitting.

The anti-budget, on the other hand, is more like intuitive eating for your wallet. It's flexible, realistic, and focused on what really matters. It's not about tracking every cent or categorizing every purchase. Instead, it's about understanding your money habits, setting meaningful goals, and making your cash work for you.

So, how does this magical anti-budget work? Glad you asked. Let's break it down.

Step 1: Know Your Numbers

The first rule of the anti-budget club is: you gotta know your numbers. But we're not talking about creating a complex spreadsheet with 57 different categories. Nope, we're keeping it simple. All you need to know is:

1. How much money comes in each month (after taxes)

2. How much goes out for fixed expenses (rent, utilities, debt payments, etc.)

3. How much is left over

That's it. Three numbers. You can literally write them on a Post-it note and stick it to your fridge. Congratulations, you now know more about your finances than most people.

Step 2: Pay Yourself First

Here's where the anti-budget starts to diverge from traditional budgeting. Instead of allocating every dollar to a specific category, we're going to focus on one key principle: pay yourself first.

Take a chunk of that leftover money – let's say 20% to start – and immediately squirrel it away into savings or investments. This is your "Future You" fund. It could be for emergencies, retirement, a down payment on a house, or your plan to become a professional beach bum in Bali. The point is, this money is off-limits for day-to-day spending.

Why is this so important? Because it flips the script on traditional budgeting. Instead of saving whatever's left at the end of the month (which, let's be honest, is usually nothing), you're prioritizing your long-term financial health right off the bat.

Step 3: Spend Your Damn Money

Now, here's the part where traditional budgeters might clutch their pearls: I want you to spend the rest of your money. Yep, you heard me right. Spend it. Enjoy it. Live your life.

But Blair, you might be thinking, isn't that irresponsible? Shouldn't I be meticulously tracking every penny?

Once you've covered your fixed expenses and paid yourself first, the rest is fair game. Want to blow it all on vintage Star Wars action figures? Go for it. Prefer to save a bit more? That's cool too. The point is, you don't need to feel guilty about your spending as long as you're meeting your savings goals.

This approach takes the stress and shame out of budgeting. No more beating yourself up for buying a latte or splurging on concert tickets. No more feeling like you need to justify every purchase. As long as you're living within your means and saving for the future, you're golden.

Step 4: Automate Everything

Listen to this little secret: willpower is overrated. Relying on willpower to manage your money is like expecting a toddler to resist a cookie jar. It might work for a while, but eventually, that cookie is being eaten.

That's why the anti-budget relies heavily on automation. Set up automatic transfers to your savings account as soon as your paycheck hits. Use apps to round up your purchases and invest the spare change. Set up automatic payments for your bills.

The less you have to actively think about managing your money, the more likely you are to stick to your plan. It's like putting your finances on autopilot – you can sit back, relax, and watch your wealth grow.

Step 5: Review and Adjust

Just because we're not tracking every penny doesn't mean we're flying blind. Once a month, take a quick look at your accounts. Are you hitting your savings goals? Are your fixed expenses creeping up? Do you feel stressed about money, or are you comfortable?

This monthly check-in is your chance to make adjustments. Maybe you realize you can save more. Maybe you decide to cut back on a subscription you're not using. The key is to stay flexible and responsive to your changing needs and goals.

Now, I know what some of you might be thinking. "But Blair, what if I'm in debt? What if I'm living paycheck to paycheck? Will this anti-budget still work for me?"

The short answer is: yes, absolutely. In fact, the anti-budget can be even more powerful for those in tight financial situations. Here's why:

1. It focuses on the big picture. When you're struggling financially, it's easy to get bogged down in the day-to-day stress of making ends meet. The anti-budget helps you zoom out and focus on your overall financial health.

2. It's not all-or-nothing. With traditional budgeting, it's easy to feel like you've failed if you don't stick to it perfectly. The anti-budget is more forgiving. Even if you can only save 1% at first, that's still a win.

3. It reduces financial stress. By automating your savings and bill payments, you're taking a lot of the daily worry out of managing your money.

4. It's adaptable. As your financial situation improves, your anti-budget can easily scale up with you.

Look, at the end of the day, the best budget is the one you'll actually stick to. If color-coded spreadsheets and detailed expense tracking work for you, that's fantastic. But if you're like most people – if you've tried traditional budgeting and found yourself falling off the wagon time and time again – then the anti-budget might be just what you need.

Remember, the goal isn't to become a penny-pinching miser who never enjoys life. The goal is to build a healthy relationship with money, to save for the future while still enjoying the present. It's about creating a system that works with your life, not against it.

So give the anti-budget a try. Start paying yourself first. Automate your finances. And for Pete's sake, buy that latte without guilt. Your future self (and your taste buds) will thank you.

TRACKING LIKE A PRO

"In God we trust. All others must bring data."

- W. Edwards Deming

As a financial advisor in the digital age, I've seen this quote take on new meaning. In a world where we can track our steps, our sleep, and even our screen time, why shouldn't we apply the same data-driven approach to our finances?

Let's face it: manually tracking every penny you spend is about as fun as watching paint dry. It's tedious, time-consuming, and let's be honest, most of us would rather binge-watch The Office for the umpteenth time than sit down with a stack of receipts and a spreadsheet.

But here's the kicker: according to a study by the National Foundation for Credit Counseling, 65% of Americans don't know how much they spent last month. That's like trying to lose weight without ever stepping on a scale. It's a recipe for financial disaster.

The good news? We're living in a golden age of financial technology. There's an app for everything, and managing your money is no exception. These digital tools can do the heavy lifting for you, turning the chore of budgeting into a seamless part of your daily life.

So, let's look at some of the financial apps and tools that can help you track your money like a pro, without losing your sanity in the process.

1. Mint: The Jack-of-All-Trades

Mint is the Swiss Army knife of budgeting apps. It's free, it's comprehensive, and it's been around long enough to work out most of its kinks. Mint automatically categorizes your transactions, tracks your spending, and even reminds you about upcoming bills.

Pros:

- Automatic transaction categorization
- Bill tracking and reminders
- Free credit score updates
- Investment tracking

Cons:

- Ads can be annoying
- Categorization isn't always accurate
- Limited customization options

Pro Tip: Take the time to customize your categories at the start. Mint's default categories are a good starting point, but tailoring them to your specific needs will make the app much more useful in the long run.

2. You Need A Budget (YNAB): The Tough Love Coach

YNAB is like that personal trainer who pushes you to do one more rep when you think you can't. It's based on the zero-based budgeting method, which means you assign every dollar a job.

Pros:

- Encourages proactive money management
- Excellent educational resources
- Detailed reporting
- Great for getting out of debt

Cons:

- Steep learning curve
- Requires more manual input than some other apps
- Subscription-based ($84/year)

Pro Tip: Take advantage of YNAB's free workshops and educational content. They're not just trying to sell you on the app; they're genuinely trying to teach you better money habits.

3. Personal Capital: The Wealth Builder

If you're more focused on investing and building wealth than day-to-day budgeting, Personal Capital is your go-to. It's like having a financial advisor in your pocket.

Pros:

- Excellent investment tracking and analysis
- Retirement planning tools
- Free to use for basic features
- Holistic view of your financial life

Cons:

- Basic budgeting features compared to dedicated budgeting apps
- Pushes their paid advisory services
- Requires a significant amount of financial data to be truly useful

Pro Tip: Use Personal Capital's "Investment Checkup" tool regularly. It compares your current portfolio allocation to an ideal target allocation based on your risk tolerance and goals.

4. Goodbudget: The Envelope System for the Digital Age

Remember the old-school envelope budgeting system your grandparents might have used? Goodbudget brings that concept into the 21st century.

Pros:

- Great for couples who want to budget together
- Helps you plan for big, irregular expenses
- Forces you to be intentional about your spending
- Free version available

Cons:

- Requires more manual input than some other apps
- Limited number of "envelopes" in the free version
- Doesn't automatically sync with your bank accounts

Pro Tip: Use Goodbudget's "Annual Envelope" feature for those once-a-year expenses that always seem to catch you off guard, like car insurance or holiday gifts.

5. Truebill: The Subscription Slayer

In an era of Netflix, Spotify, and a million other monthly subscriptions, Truebill helps you keep track of where your money is going and cancels subscriptions you no longer want.

Pros:

- Automatically finds and categorizes your subscriptions
- Can negotiate bills on your behalf
- Tracks spending and provides insights
- Free version available

Cons:

- Takes a cut of the money they save you on bill negotiations
- Some features require the premium version
- Limited budgeting features compared to dedicated budgeting apps

Pro Tip: Use Truebill's bill negotiation feature for your cable and internet bills. These companies often have unadvertised promotions that Truebill can help you access.

Now, here's the million-dollar question: which app should you use?

The truth is, the best app is the one you'll actually use consistently. It's like picking a workout routine - the most effective one is the one you'll stick with.

My advice? Start with Mint if you're new to budgeting apps. It's free, it's comprehensive, and it does a lot of the work for you. If you find yourself wanting more control and don't mind putting in a bit more effort, give YNAB a shot. For those focused on investing and long-term wealth building, Personal Capital is hard to beat.

Whichever app you choose, here are some universal tips to help you make the most of it:

1. Link all your accounts: The more comprehensive your financial picture, the more useful these apps become.
2. Check in regularly: Set a weekly "money date" with yourself to review your finances. Make it enjoyable - brew your favorite coffee, put on some good music, and dive in.
3. Use the mobile app: The easier it is to check your finances on the go, the more likely you are to stay on top of things.
4. Set realistic goals: Start small and work your way up. It's better to consistently save $50 a month than to aim for $500 and give up after a month.
5. Be patient: It takes time to build new habits. Stick with it for at least three months before deciding if an app is right for you.

Remember, these apps are tools, not magic wands. They can provide incredible insights and make managing your money much easier, but they can't make financial decisions for you. You're still in the driver's seat.

The beauty of these tools is that they turn your financial life into a game you can win. They provide real-time feedback, celebrate your victories (however small), and help you visualize your progress towards your goals.

So, pick an app, link your accounts, and start tracking.

CHAPTER 4

SLAYING THE STUDENT LOAN DRAGON (AND OTHER BEASTS)

THE LOAN RANGER

"Education is the most powerful weapon which you can use to change the world." - **Nelson Mandela**

Yeah, yeah, I know. You've probably seen that quote plastered on every motivational poster from here to Timbuktu. But here's what Mandela left out: that weapon comes with a hefty price tag, and for many of us, it's called student debt.

Let's start with a reality check: as of 2023, Americans owe a staggering $1.75 trillion in student loan debt. That's trillion with a T, folks. To put that in perspective, that's enough money to buy about 5.8 billion iPhones or 437.5 million years of Netflix subscriptions. (Not that I'm suggesting you blow your loan money on binge-watching and gadgets, mind you.)

If you're reading this with a knot in your stomach, wondering how you're going to pay off your own personal chunk of that $1.75 trillion, take a deep breath. I've got your back. As someone who's spent years helping people untangle the Gordian knot of student loans, I'm here to tell you: it's complicated, it's frustrating, but it's not hopeless.

Types of Student Loans: Federal vs. Private

First things first: not all student loans are created equal. There are two main types: federal and private.

Federal loans are like that dependable friend who always has your back. They're issued by the government and come with a range of benefits and protections. These include:

1. Fixed interest rates
2. Income-driven repayment plans
3. Potential loan forgiveness
4. Deferment and forbearance options

Private loans, on the other hand, are more like that sketchy cousin who borrows money and conveniently "forgets" to pay you back. They're issued by banks, credit unions, or other private lenders, and they typically offer:

1. Variable or fixed interest rates (often higher than federal loans)
2. Fewer repayment options
3. Less flexibility if you run into financial trouble

If you have a mix of federal and private loans, always, always, ALWAYS prioritize your federal loans. They're like the VIPs of the student loan world – treat them accordingly.

Repayment Plans

When it comes to federal loans, you've got options. It's like a "Choose Your Own Adventure" book, except instead of fighting dragons or exploring haunted houses, you're battling interest rates and exploring repayment plans. Fun, right?

Here are the main repayment plans for federal loans:

1. Standard Repayment Plan: This is the default option. You pay a fixed amount each month for up to 10 years. It's simple, but it can mean higher monthly payments.

2. Graduated Repayment Plan: Your payments start low and increase every two years. This plan assumes your income will grow over time. (Spoiler alert: life doesn't always work that way.)

3. Extended Repayment Plan: This stretches your repayment period up to 25 years, lowering your monthly payments but increasing the total amount you'll pay over time.

4. Income-Driven Repayment Plans: These are the real MVPs of the repayment world. Your monthly payment is based on your income and family size.

There are four types:

- Income-Based Repayment (IBR)
- Pay As You Earn (PAYE)
- Revised Pay As You Earn (REPAYE)
- Income-Contingent Repayment (ICR)

These plans can significantly lower your monthly payments, and any remaining balance is forgiven after 20-25 years. However, you'll need to recertify your income and family size annually.

Pro tip: If you're pursuing Public Service Loan Forgiveness (more on that later), you MUST be on an income-driven plan. Don't learn this the hard way after 10 years of payments. Trust me, I've seen the tears.

Loan Forgiveness: The Holy Grail

Ah, loan forgiveness. It's the unicorn of the student loan world – magical, elusive, and often misunderstood. There are several forgiveness programs, but the two big ones are:

1. ***Public Service Loan Forgiveness (PSLF):*** If you work for a government organization or non-profit, you might be eligible for PSLF. After making 120

qualifying payments (that's 10 years of payments, folks), your remaining balance is forgiven. Tax-free.

2. **Teacher Loan Forgiveness:** If you teach full-time for five consecutive years in a low-income school, you may be eligible for forgiveness of up to $17,500 on your Direct Subsidized and Unsubsidized Loans.

Sounds great, right? Well, here's where I need to hit you with some tough love: forgiveness programs are notoriously difficult to qualify for. As of 2021, only about 2% of PSLF applications were approved. That's not a typo. Two percent.

But don't let that discourage you! If you think you might qualify, go for it. Just make sure you're crossing every 't' and dotting every 'i'. Keep meticulous records, submit your Employment Certification Form annually, and stay on top of any program changes.

Strategies for Taming the Loan Beast

Alright, now that we've covered the basics, let's talk strategy. Here are some tried-and-true methods for getting those loans under control:

1. The Avalanche Method: Target the loan with the highest interest rate first. This saves you the most

money in the long run. It's like killing the biggest, baddest monster in the dungeon first.

2. The Snowball Method: Start with the smallest loan and work your way up. This gives you quick wins and can be motivating. It's like clearing out all the little goblins before taking on the dragon.
3. Refinancing: This can be a good option if you have private loans or if you're confident you won't need the protections of federal loans. But be careful – refinancing federal loans turns them private, and you lose all those sweet federal benefits.
4. Extra Payments: Any extra money you can throw at your loans will help. Even an extra $20 a month can make a difference over time. It's like chipping away at a mountain – every little bit counts.
5. Autopay: Many lenders offer an interest rate reduction (usually 0.25%) if you set up automatic payments. It's not much, but hey, every little bit helps.

Negotiating with Lenders: It's Not You, It's Them

Lenders are people too. (Well, corporations run by people, but you get the idea.) And they'd rather get some money from you than no money. If you're struggling, don't be afraid to reach out and negotiate.

For federal loans, this might mean switching to an income-driven plan or applying for deferment or forbearance. For private loans, you might be able to negotiate a lower interest rate or a temporary reduction in payments.

The key is to be proactive. Don't wait until you're missing payments to reach out. Be honest about your situation, have a plan, and don't be afraid to advocate for yourself.

The Emotional Toll

Let's get real for a moment: student debt isn't just a financial burden. It's an emotional one too. It can affect your mental health, your relationships, even your life decisions. Should you take that dream job that pays less? Can you afford to start a family? Buy a house? Take a vacation without feeling guilty?

These are heavy questions, and there's no one-size-fits-all answer. But here's what I can tell you: you are more than your debt. Your worth as a person is not determined by the number on your loan statement.

Yes, take your debt seriously. Yes, make a plan to pay it off. But don't let it consume you. Remember why you took on this debt in the first place – to invest in yourself, in your education, in your future.

And remember, you're not alone in this. Millions of people are in the same boat. Don't be afraid to reach out for help, whether that's to a financial advisor, a therapist, or just a friend who's willing to listen.

Look, I'm not going to sugar-coat it: paying off student loans is a long, often frustrating journey. There will be times when you feel like you're not making progress, when you're tempted to just ignore those statements piling up in your inbox.

But here's the thing: you've got this. You're smart (hey, you went to college, right?), you're resourceful (you found this book, didn't you?), and you're willing to learn and take action. That puts you ahead of the game already.

Stay informed, stay proactive, and most importantly, stay hopeful. Your education is an investment in yourself, and like any investment, it takes time to pay off. But it will pay off, in ways both financial and personal.

DEBT SNOWBALL VS. AVALANCHE

"In the fight against debt, it's not the size of the weapon that matters, but the strategy behind it."

Debt is an adversary that creeps up quietly, accumulating over time until it feels like you're surrounded on all sides. Whether it's credit card debt, student loans, or personal loans, the key to winning the battle is not just about the size of your paycheck, but the strategy you deploy. Two of the most effective strategies are the Debt Snowball and Debt Avalanche methods. These approaches are your weapons in the fight to reclaim your financial freedom. Each has its own strengths and weaknesses, and like any good general, you need to know when and how to deploy them.

Before we dive into battle tactics, let's get clear on the weapons at your disposal.

Debt Snowball Method:

The Debt Snowball method is all about momentum. You start by paying off your smallest debts first, regardless of interest rates, while making minimum payments on your larger debts. As each small debt is paid off, you take the money you were paying on that debt and roll it into the next smallest debt. This creates a "snowball" effect, where your payments grow larger as you move from one debt to the next.

Debt Avalanche Method:

The Debt Avalanche method is more precise and calculated. In this strategy, you target the debt with the highest interest rate first, while making minimum payments on your other debts. Once the highest-interest debt is paid off, you move to the next highest, and so on. This method minimizes the amount of interest you pay over time, making it financially efficient.

Battle Tactics: How Each Method Works

Debt Snowball in Action:

Imagine you have four debts:

1. $500 on a credit card at 5% interest
2. $2,000 on a personal loan at 10% interest
3. $7,000 on a car loan at 8% interest
4. $15,000 in student loans at 6% interest

With the Debt Snowball method, you focus on paying off the $500 credit card debt first, while making minimum payments on the other three. Let's say you can afford to put $150 extra towards your debt each month. You would:

- Pay the $25 minimum on the credit card, plus the extra $150, making it $175 per month.
- Continue making the minimum payments on the other debts.

In just under three months, that credit card debt is gone. Now, you take that $175 and add it to the $60 minimum payment you were making on your personal loan. You're now paying $235 a month on the personal loan, while still making minimum payments on the car loan and student loans. As each debt is eliminated, the snowball grows, and before you know it, you're tackling the larger debts with a powerful payment.

Debt Avalanche in Action:

Now, let's flip the script and look at the Debt Avalanche method with the same four debts:

1. $500 on a credit card at 5% interest
2. $2,000 on a personal loan at 10% interest
3. $7,000 on a car loan at 8% interest
4. $15,000 in student loans at 6% interest

Here, you'll focus on the $2,000 personal loan first because it has the highest interest rate. You apply the $150 extra to this debt, paying $210 per month ($150 extra plus the $60 minimum). Once that's paid off, you move to the $7,000 car loan, then the student loans, and finally the credit card debt.

This method saves you money in interest over time. However, the emotional reward isn't as immediate since you don't experience the quick wins of eliminating small debts early on.

Pros and Cons: Choosing Your Battlefield

Debt Snowball Pros:

- **Psychological Victory:** Paying off smaller debts quickly provides a psychological boost. It's like taking out the enemy's front line—your confidence grows with each small victory.
- **Momentum:** The snowball effect creates a sense of momentum. As you pay off each debt, you have more money to throw at the next one, making it easier to stay motivated.

Debt Snowball Cons:

- **Cost:** By focusing on the smallest debts rather than the highest interest rates, you might pay more in interest over the long term. This approach sacrifices some financial efficiency for emotional satisfaction.

- **Slow Progress on Big Debts:** Large debts can feel like a slow grind when you finally reach them. After the initial victories, the battle against larger debts may seem endless.

Debt Avalanche Pros:

- **Financial Efficiency:** By attacking the highest-interest debts first, you minimize the amount of money lost to interest. This is the financially smarter choice in the long term.
- **Clear Plan:** The Debt Avalanche method is based on numbers, not emotions. For those who can stay disciplined, it's the more logical approach.

Debt Avalanche Cons:

- **Delayed Satisfaction:** You don't get the quick wins that the Debt Snowball offers. The first few months (or even years) might feel like you're barely making a dent, which can be discouraging.
- **Requires Discipline:** Without the psychological boost of early victories, it can be harder to stay motivated. This method requires a high level of self-discipline.

The War Stories: Clients Who Triumphed

Let me tell you about Sergeant Maria, a client who came to me drowning in $50,000 of debt. She had credit cards, personal loans, and a car loan, all weighing her down like heavy combat gear.

We started with the Debt Snowball. Maria was skeptical at first - "How is paying off this tiny $500 credit card going to help?" she asked. But two months later, when that first debt was wiped out, I saw a change in her. There was a glint in her eye, a straightening of her spine. She was ready for more.

Over the next year, Maria knocked out three more small debts. Her confidence grew with each victory. But then we hit a roadblock - the remaining debts were large and had high interest rates. Maria's motivation began to flag.

That's when we switched tactics. We transitioned to the Debt Avalanche, focusing on her 22% APR credit card. It was a slog - month after month of payments with little visible progress. But Maria had tasted victory, and she wasn't about to surrender.

Two years into our campaign, Maria had reduced her debt by 60%. That's when life threw a curveball - she received an unexpected $5,000 bonus at work. In the past, Maria *might have splurged on a vacation or a shopping spree. But not this Maria. No, this battle-hardened warrior put every cent toward her highest-interest debt.*

That bonus was like calling in an air strike. It decimated her largest credit card balance and gave her campaign a massive boost.

Three years and seven months after we began, Maria made her final debt payment. She was free.

Choosing between the Debt Snowball and Debt Avalanche methods depends on your personality, financial situation, and the nature of your debts. If you're someone who needs quick victories to stay motivated, the Debt Snowball might be your best bet. It's about building momentum and morale, keeping your spirits high as you cut down each enemy, one by one.

However, if you're more disciplined and driven by logic and long-term savings, the Debt Avalanche could be the way to go. It's the strategy of the cold, calculating general who doesn't care about the small skirmishes but is focused on winning the war with minimal losses.

Debt is a formidable opponent, but with the right strategy, it's one you can defeat. Whether you choose the Debt Snowball or Debt Avalanche, the most important thing is that you have a plan and stick to it. This is a battle of attrition, requiring perseverance and commitment. But every dollar you pay off is one step closer to victory. The battlefield may be tough, but with the right weapon in your hand, there's no debt too large, no obstacle too great. Victory is within your grasp—now go claim it.

CHAPTER 5

THE EMERGENCY FUND

FROM ZERO TO HERO: BUILDING YOUR FIRST $1,000 SAFETY NET

"It's not about how much money you make, but how much money you keep." — **Robert Kiyosaki**

Reframe Your Mindset: Viewing Savings as a Game

Saving money can often feel like a chore, but what if you approached it like a game? Imagine each dollar saved as a point scored in a financial game where your ultimate goal is to reach $1,000. This shift in perspective can make the process more engaging and less stressful. Set up personal challenges, like seeing how many no-spend days you can string together or finding creative ways to cut costs.

Cash in on Hidden Talents

Everyone has a unique skill or hobby that can be monetized. Whether you're great at photography, know how to fix things around the house, or have a knack for writing, there's likely a market for your talents. Start by offering your services to friends and family, and then expand to online platforms like Etsy, TaskRabbit, or Upwork. These side gigs can bring in extra cash without requiring a major time commitment, allowing you to steadily grow your savings.

The "Round-Up" Strategy

A simple yet effective method to accelerate your savings is the round-up strategy. This involves rounding up your everyday purchases to the nearest dollar and saving the difference. For example, if you spend $4.50 on coffee, round it up to $5 and put that extra $0.50 into your savings. Many banking apps now offer automatic round-up features, making this an effortless way to accumulate savings over time.

The Art of Bartering

Bartering, an age-old practice, can be surprisingly effective in modern times. Instead of spending money on goods or services, consider what you can trade. For instance, you might offer dog-walking services in exchange for a haircut or trade your baking skills for someone's gardening help. This not only saves money but also create a sense of community and mutual support.

The One-In, One-Out Rule

To avoid unnecessary purchases and declutter your life, adopt the one-in, one-out rule. For every new item you buy, sell or donate something you already own. This practice forces you to think critically about what you truly need, and the money you make from selling items can be added directly to your savings.

Turn Found Money into Savings

Found money—unexpected windfalls like birthday cash, tax refunds, or bonuses—can be a great boost to your emergency fund. Instead of spending it impulsively, commit to saving at least 50% (or ideally all) of any found money. This can quickly propel you toward your $1,000 goal without disrupting your daily budget.

Start a "No-Spend" Challenge

A no-spend challenge is a powerful way to reset your spending habits and jumpstart your savings. Pick a timeframe—whether it's a weekend, a week, or even a month—and commit to spending money only on absolute necessities like groceries, rent, and utilities. The money you don't spend during this challenge can be funneled directly into your savings.

Passive Income Through Investment Apps

Consider making your money work for you by exploring micro-investing apps like Acorns or Stash, which allow you to invest small amounts of money and earn passive income over time. While this isn't a quick-fix solution, the returns on your investments can contribute to your savings goals in the long run.

The Community-Supported Fund

Sometimes, achieving your financial goals is easier with support from your community. Consider organizing a "savings circle" with friends or family members who are also looking to build their emergency funds. Each person contributes a small, manageable amount to the group fund each week, and one member receives the total each time. This method provides both accountability and encouragement, making the savings process more communal and less isolating.

Utilize Cashback and Reward Programs

Take advantage of cashback apps, credit card rewards, and loyalty programs that offer money back on purchases you're already making. Redirect the cash rewards or points you earn straight into your savings account. Over time, these small amounts can add up to significant savings.

The Power of Perspective: It's Not Just About the Money

Finally, remember that building your first $1,000 safety net is not just about the money—it's about developing the discipline and mindset that will carry you through all your financial endeavors. The process of saving teaches you to be resourceful, patient, and resilient. These qualities will serve you well as you continue to build your financial future.

LEVELING UP: STRATEGIES FOR A FULLY-FUNDED EMERGENCY ACCOUNT

"The best time to plant a tree was twenty years ago. The second-best time is now." — **Chinese Proverb**

When it comes to building a fully-funded emergency account, this timeless wisdom rings true. An emergency fund is your financial safety net, the foundation that ensures you can weather life's storms without falling into debt or financial ruin. But the question remains: How much should you save, and how do you get there?

Determining the Right Size for Your Emergency Fund

The size of your emergency fund depends on several factors, including your income, expenses, dependents, and overall financial stability. The general rule of thumb is to save enough to cover three to six months' worth of living expenses. However, this is just a starting point.

1. **Consider Your Income Stability:** If you have a steady job with a reliable income, three months' worth of expenses might suffice. But if you're self-employed, work in a volatile industry, or have variable income, aim for six to twelve months' worth of expenses. The more uncertain your income, the larger your emergency fund should be.

2. **Account for Dependents:** If you have children, elderly parents, or others who rely on your income, your emergency fund should be on the higher end of the spectrum. Additional dependents mean additional expenses, so it's crucial to have a cushion that can support your entire household.

3. **Factor in Health and Insurance:** Consider your health and any insurance coverage you have. If you have a history of medical issues or inadequate health insurance, it's wise to save more to cover potential medical emergencies.

4. **Evaluate Your Debt Situation:** If you have high-interest debt, you might want to strike a balance between paying down debt and building your emergency fund. However, having at least one

month's worth of expenses saved before aggressively tackling debt is essential.

Setting a Realistic Goal

Once you've determined the size of your emergency fund, break it down into manageable goals. If you need to save $18,000 to cover six months of expenses, set milestones like $3,000, $6,000, $12,000, and so on. This not only makes the goal seem less daunting but also allows you to celebrate your progress along the way.

Choosing the Right Savings Vehicles

Your emergency fund should be accessible, but that doesn't mean it should sit idle. Here's how to balance liquidity with growth:

1. **High-Yield Savings Accounts:** This is the most common place to stash your emergency fund. High-yield savings accounts offer better interest rates than traditional savings accounts while keeping your money easily accessible. Look for accounts with no fees and easy online access.

2. **Money Market Accounts:** These accounts typically offer higher interest rates than regular savings accounts, along with check-writing privileges. They're a good option if you want to keep your

emergency fund separate from your everyday spending money while still earning interest.

3. **Certificates of Deposit (CDs):** If you're confident you won't need to touch your emergency fund for a while, consider a CD. While CDs provide higher interest rates, they also come with penalties for early withdrawal. A strategy known as CD laddering—buying multiple CDs with different maturity dates—can provide liquidity while maximizing returns.

4. **Cash Management Accounts:** Offered by brokerage firms, these accounts combine features of checking, savings, and investment accounts. They often come with higher interest rates and FDIC insurance, making them a solid choice for an emergency fund.

5. **Savings Bonds:** While not as liquid as other options, U.S. savings bonds can be a part of a diversified emergency fund strategy. Series I bonds, in particular, offer inflation protection and can serve as a long-term backup to your more liquid savings.

Building Your Fund: Strategies for Success

Building a fully-funded emergency account takes time and discipline. Let me show you how you can stay on track:

1. **Automate Your Savings:** Set up automatic transfers from your checking account to your emergency fund. This makes saving a priority and ensures you consistently contribute without having to think about it.

2. **Boost Your Income:** Consider picking up a side hustle or freelancing to accelerate your savings. Even a few extra hours a week can make a significant difference over time.

3. **Reduce Unnecessary Expenses:** Conduct a thorough review of your spending habits and cut back on non-essential expenses. Redirect that money into your emergency fund.

4. **Use Windfalls Wisely:** Whenever you receive unexpected money—whether it's a tax refund, bonus, or gift—put a substantial portion of it into your emergency fund. This can give your savings a significant boost.

5. **Prioritize Your Emergency Fund Over Luxuries:** It's tempting to spend on vacations, new gadgets, or dining out, but prioritizing your emergency fund will pay off in the long run. Remind yourself that the

peace of mind that comes with financial security is worth more than short-term pleasures.

Resisting the Temptation to Dip Into Your Fund

An emergency fund is just that—a fund for emergencies. But the temptation to use it for non-essential purchases or "special occasions" can be strong. How, then can you resist it:

1. **Create a Clear Definition of Emergencies:** Before building your fund, define what constitutes an emergency. Unexpected medical bills, car repairs, or job loss qualify; a new TV or vacation does not. Write down your rules and stick to them.

2. **Keep It Out of Sight:** Consider keeping your emergency fund in a separate bank from your everyday accounts. Out of sight, out of mind. This reduces the temptation to dip into it for non-emergencies.

3. **Establish a Waiting Period:** If you're tempted to use your emergency fund, implement a 48-hour waiting period. This gives you time to evaluate whether the expense is truly necessary or if it can be handled through other means.

4. **Have a Backup Plan:** Create a secondary fund for unexpected, non-emergency expenses—like car maintenance or holiday gifts. This "sinking fund" helps protect your emergency savings.

Building a fully-funded emergency account is more than just a financial goal; it's a commitment to long-term stability and peace of mind. It's about ensuring that you and your loved ones are protected from life's inevitable uncertainties.

CHAPTER 6

INVESTING FOR THE CLUELESS

DEMYSTIFYING THE STOCK MARKET

"The stock market is a device for transferring money from the impatient to the patient." — **Warren Buffett**

Investing in the stock market often feels like stepping into a mysterious world full of complicated terms and intimidating numbers. But what if I told you that at its core, the stock market is simply a place where people buy and sell pieces of companies? Let's strip away the jargon and get to the heart of what you really need to know to start investing confidently.

What Are Stocks?

Imagine you and a few friends decide to start a lemonade stand. To get it off the ground, you each put in some money and agree to split the profits. In the business world, when a company wants to grow, it often needs more money than the founders can provide on their own. So, they sell shares—little pieces of ownership in the company—to the public. Each share you buy represents a tiny slice of the company and its potential profits.

Owning a stock means you have a claim on a portion of the company's assets and earnings. If the company does well, the value of your stock could increase, and you might even receive dividends—a share of the company's profits. But if the company struggles, the value of your stock could drop.

Bonds: The Lender's Path

If owning a piece of a company sounds exciting, imagine this: instead of owning part of the lemonade stand, what if you lent them money to buy more lemons, with the promise that they'd pay you back with interest? That's essentially what bonds are.

When companies or governments need to raise money, they can issue bonds. By buying a bond, you're lending money to the issuer for a set period. In return, they agree to pay you interest at regular intervals and return your principal—the original amount you invested—when the bond matures.

Bonds are generally considered safer than stocks because they offer fixed interest payments and the return of your principal. However, their returns are usually lower than stocks over the long term. They're like the dependable, steady part of your investment portfolio.

Mutual Funds: Pooling Resources for Bigger Gains

Now, suppose your lemonade stand grew into a chain of stands, and you wanted to spread out your investment risk by owning shares in various stands instead of just one. But researching and buying individual shares for each stand seems overwhelming. This is where mutual funds come in.

A mutual fund is like a basket filled with a variety of stocks, bonds, or other securities. When you invest in a mutual fund, you pool your money with other investors, and a professional manager selects and manages the investments in the fund. This allows you to diversify—spread out your investments—without having to pick individual stocks or bonds yourself.

Mutual funds can be tailored to various goals. Some might focus on growth by investing in stocks, while others might aim for income by investing in bonds. The idea is that by spreading your investments across multiple assets, you reduce the risk of losing money if one investment performs poorly.

ETFs: The Flexibility of a Stock, the Diversity of a Fund

Exchange-traded funds (ETFs) are like a modern twist on mutual funds. Think of an ETF as a mutual fund that trades like a stock. ETFs hold a collection of assets—like stocks, bonds, or commodities—just like mutual funds, but they can be bought and sold throughout the day on the stock market, just like individual stocks.

This means you get the best of both worlds: the diversification of a mutual fund and the flexibility of a stock. ETFs often have lower fees than mutual funds and offer a convenient way to invest in a broad market index, like the S&P 500, which tracks the performance of 500 of the largest companies in the U.S.

Common Fears and Misconceptions

The stock market can seem like a rollercoaster—full of ups and downs that might make you queasy. But let's address some common fears and misconceptions to help you feel more confident:

1. **"The Stock Market Is Too Risky":** Yes, investing in the stock market involves risk. But risk and reward go hand in hand. Historically, the stock market has outperformed other types of investments, like bonds or savings accounts, over the long term. The key is to think long-term and not panic when the market dips.

2. **"I Need a Lot of Moncy to Start":** This is a myth. Thanks to modern technology, you can start investing with just a few dollars. Many platforms allow you to buy fractional shares, meaning you can invest in

expensive stocks like Amazon or Tesla with whatever amount you're comfortable with.

3. **"I Don't Know Enough to Invest":** The truth is, you don't need to be a financial expert to start investing. Begin with the basics—like understanding stocks, bonds, mutual funds, and ETFs—and build your knowledge over time. Start small, stay curious, and learn as you go.

4. **"I'll Lose All My Money":** While the stock market does have risks, diversification and smart investing can help protect your money. By spreading your investments across different asset types and industries, you reduce the chances of losing everything. Also, remember that investing is a marathon, not a sprint. The market may fluctuate, but historically, it has trended upwards over time.

Let's look at a real-world example to illustrate how the market works. Imagine two friends, Janae and Tom. Janae starts investing $100 a month in an S&P 500 index fund at age 25. Tom waits until he's 35 to start but invests $200 a month to catch up. By the time they're both 65, who do you think has more money?

Despite investing less each month, Janae ends up with more because her money had more time to grow. This is the power of compounding—earning returns on your returns. The longer your money stays invested, the more it can grow.

The stock market doesn't require a degree in finance; it just requires the willingness to learn and the courage to start. Think of it like planting a tree: the sooner you start, the sooner you'll see it grow.

Begin with small, consistent investments, and remember that it's okay to feel uncertain at first. Like anything new, investing takes time to get comfortable with. But with patience and persistence, you'll build the knowledge and confidence needed to grow your wealth over time.

BEYOND STOCKS: EXPLORING REAL ESTATE, BONDS, AND MORE

"Don't put all your eggs in one basket." — This age-old proverb has never been more relevant than when it comes to investing. While stocks are a popular investment vehicle, they are far from the only option available. In fact, diversifying your portfolio beyond stocks can provide stability, potential growth, and even some financial surprises. Let's look at the various investment options beyond the stock market, including real estate, bonds, peer-to-peer lending, and other alternatives, so you can make informed decisions about where to put your money.

Real estate is often seen as a cornerstone of wealth building. Unlike stocks, real estate provides something tangible—you can see and touch the property you own, and it tends to appreciate in value over time. There are several ways to invest in real estate, from purchasing rental properties to investing in **Real Estate Investment Trusts (REITs)**.

Rental Properties: Purchasing rental properties involves buying homes or commercial spaces and renting them out to tenants. The main advantage is the potential for steady, passive income. If you've chosen the right location, your property may also appreciate, providing long-term capital gains. However, being a landlord comes with its challenges—dealing with tenants, maintenance, and unexpected vacancies can be time-consuming and stressful.

REITs: If managing a property isn't appealing, REITs offer a more hands-off approach to real estate investing. A REIT is a company that owns, operates, or finances income-producing real estate across various sectors. Investing in REITs allows you to benefit from real estate investments without directly owning property. They provide dividends and tend to be less volatile than stocks. However, the returns may be lower than directly owning property, and REITs are subject to market risks.

Pros of Real Estate:

- Tangible asset
- Potential for regular income (through rent)
- Tax benefits (like deductions for mortgage interest)

Cons of Real Estate:

- High entry costs
- Maintenance and management responsibilities

- Market risks (property value can fluctuate)

Bonds: The Steady Path to Income

Bonds are often described as the bedrock of a conservative investment portfolio. When you buy a bond, you're essentially lending money to a government or corporation for a fixed period, during which you receive regular interest payments. At the end of the term, the bond matures, and the issuer returns your principal amount.

There are several types of bonds, including **government bonds** (like U.S. Treasuries), **municipal bonds** (issued by local governments), and **corporate bonds** (issued by companies). Each type comes with varying levels of risk and return. Generally, government bonds are the safest but give lower returns, while corporate bonds provide higher returns but come with more risk.

Pros of Bonds:

- Stable, predictable income (through interest payments)
- Lower risk compared to stocks
- Diversification benefits (they often perform well when stocks do poorly)

Cons of Bonds:

- Lower returns compared to stocks
- Interest rate risk (bond prices can drop when interest rates rise)
- Credit risk (corporate bonds can default if the company fails)

Peer-to-Peer Lending

Peer-to-peer (P2P) lending is a relatively new investment avenue, allowing you to lend money directly to individuals or small businesses through online platforms. In return, you earn interest on the loans. P2P lending cuts out traditional financial institutions, potentially offering higher returns than bonds or savings accounts. However, with higher returns come higher risks, as borrowers may default on their loans.

Pros of Peer-to-Peer Lending:

- Potential for higher returns
- Diversification away from traditional assets
- Ability to invest small amounts in multiple loans to spread risk

Cons of Peer-to-Peer Lending:

- Higher default risk
- Less liquidity (it may be harder to sell your investment quickly)
- Limited regulatory oversight

Alternative Investments

If you're looking for something outside the conventional, there are several **alternative investments** worth considering, each with its own unique risk and reward profile.

Precious Metals: Investing in gold, silver, or other precious metals can act as a hedge against inflation and economic instability. These assets tend to retain value during times of market volatility, but they don't generate income like stocks or bonds. The value of precious metals is also highly dependent on market demand.

Commodities: Commodities include natural resources like oil, gas, and agricultural products. Investing in commodities can offer protection against inflation, as prices often rise during inflationary periods. However, commodities can be highly volatile and are influenced by factors like weather, geopolitical events, and supply-demand imbalances.

Cryptocurrency: Cryptocurrencies like Bitcoin and Ethereum have garnered significant attention as alternative investments. While they have the potential for high returns, they are extremely volatile and speculative. Investing in cryptocurrency requires a strong risk tolerance and a willingness to accept potential losses.

Pros of Alternative Investments:

- Potential for high returns
- Diversification beyond traditional assets
- Some, like gold or commodities, provide a hedge against inflation

Cons of Alternative Investments:

- High volatility and risk
- Lack of income generation (in most cases)
- Complexity and need for specialized knowledge

Balancing Your Investment Portfolio

With so many options beyond the stock market, the key to successful investing is balance. A well-rounded portfolio might include a mix of stocks, bonds, real estate, and alternative investments. This approach allows you to capture the growth potential of stocks while enjoying the stability of bonds and the diversification offered by real estate and alternative assets.

When deciding how to allocate your investments, consider your financial goals, risk tolerance, and investment horizon. For example, a young investor with a high-risk tolerance might allocate more to stocks and alternative investments, while someone nearing retirement might focus on bonds and real estate for income and stability.

The Temptation to Go All-In

It can be tempting to go all-in on a particular investment, especially if it's performing well. But remember, the most successful investors understand the value of diversification. By spreading your investments across different asset classes, you protect yourself against the inevitable ups and downs of the market.

CHAPTER 7

THE SIDE HUSTLE REVOLUTION

FINDING YOUR NICHE

"The best way to predict the future is to create it." – **Peter Drucker**

In a world where traditional 9-to-5 jobs no longer guarantee financial security, side hustles have become the gateway to not only extra income but also personal fulfillment and financial freedom. The rise of the gig economy, the explosion of online business opportunities, and the flourishing of creative fields mean that anyone with passion, skills, and a bit of grit can turn their dreams into reality. This is not about trading your time for pennies; it's about finding that sweet spot where your talents meet market demand—a niche that not only fills your pockets but also enriches your life.

The gig economy alone is projected to generate over $455 billion by 2024, and it's only growing. Whether you're looking at driving for a rideshare company, freelancing your design skills, or launching an online shop, the opportunities are vast and varied.

But where do you start? It begins with self-discovery and market research. You don't want to waste time on gigs that don't align with your interests or have limited earning potential. Instead, the goal is to identify side hustles that not only match your skillset but also have the potential to scale.

Step 1: Assess Your Skills, Passions, and Interests

The first step is to take inventory of your strengths, passions, and interests. What are you good at? What do you love doing? What would you do for free if money weren't an issue? These are crucial questions because a successful side hustle often lies at the intersection of skill, passion, and demand.

Your side gig should feel like an extension of who you are, not a chore. It's something that should excite you and make you look forward to the hours you invest in it.

Step 2: Explore the Gig Economy and Popular Side Hustles

Once you've identified your core strengths and passions, it's time to look at the gig economy and popular side hustles. The beauty of the gig economy is its diversity. Whether you're interested in tech, arts, or manual labor, there's something out there for everyone.

1. **Freelancing:** Platforms like Upwork, Fiverr, and Toptal have democratized access to freelance work. If you're a skilled writer, designer, coder, or marketer, you can start offering your services to clients worldwide.

Freelancing provides flexibility in terms of hours and projects, and if you're good at what you do, the earning potential is substantial.

2. E-commerce: The rise of platforms like Etsy, Shopify, and Amazon has made it easier than ever to start an online store. Whether you're into crafting handmade goods, dropshipping, or selling digital products like e-books (like this one you are reading) or online courses, e-commerce is a fertile ground for turning your passions into profit.

3. Gig-based Jobs: If you prefer more physical work or enjoy meeting people, consider gig-based jobs like driving for Uber, delivering groceries for Instacart, or renting out your spare room on Airbnb. While these gigs might not scale as easily as online businesses, they offer quick cash and flexibility.

4. Creative Fields: If you're artistically inclined, consider side gigs in the creative industries. This could range from graphic design, video editing, music production, or even content creation for YouTube or TikTok. The digital age has made it possible to monetize creativity in ways that were unimaginable just a decade ago.

5. Consulting and Coaching: If you have expertise in a particular field, consider offering consulting or coaching services. This could be anything from financial advising, career coaching, or even personal training. Consulting allows you to leverage your existing knowledge to help others while earning a significant income.

Step 3: Evaluate Profitability and Sustainability

Not all side hustles are created equal. Some may give you quick cash but fizzle out in a few months, while others have the potential to grow into full-time businesses. It's essential to evaluate the profitability and sustainability of your chosen side hustle before diving in.

Let me give you some simple framework to help you assess potential side hustles:

1. Market Demand: Is there a demand for your product or service? Use tools like Google Trends, Keyword Planner, or even a simple social media search to gauge interest in your niche. If there's already a significant market, that's a good sign.

2. Competition: Analyze your competition. If the market is saturated, it might be challenging to stand out. However, if you can create something unique or better, there's always room for success. Differentiation is key.

3. Start-up Costs: How much will it cost to get started? Some side hustles require little to no upfront investment, while others might need a significant financial commitment. Make sure you're prepared to handle these costs without jeopardizing your financial stability.

4. Time Commitment: Consider how much time you can realistically dedicate to your side gig. Some hustles require more time investment upfront, while others can be managed with a few hours a week. Make sure your side hustle fits within your existing schedule without causing burnout.

5. Scalability: Can your side hustle grow? Look for opportunities that allow you to scale your efforts. For example, if you start a freelance writing gig, consider creating a blog or an e-book to reach a broader audience. The goal is to build something that can grow beyond just trading time for money.

6. Passion Alignment: Finally, does this side hustle align with your passions and values? A profitable side gig should be something you enjoy doing. If it feels like a burden, you're less likely to stick with it long-term.

Step 4: Take Action

The final step is to take action. All the planning in the world won't amount to anything unless you take the first step. Start small, test the waters, and learn as you go. Don't be afraid to fail; every misstep is a lesson that brings you closer to success.

Remember, the most successful side hustles often start as simple ideas, pursued with passion and persistence. Whether you're looking to pay off debt, save for a big purchase, or eventually replace your full-time job, a side hustle can be the key to unlocking your financial potential.

So, what are you waiting for? The perfect side gig is out there waiting for you to discover it.

FROM HOBBY TO EMPIRE: SCALING YOUR SIDE HUSTLE

"Success usually comes to those who are too busy to be looking for it." – **Henry David Thoreau**

Building a side hustle is no small feat, but scaling that side hustle into a full-fledged business? That's where the magic happens. Yet, it's also where many falter. The transition from hobby to empire demands not only passion and persistence but also a strategic approach that balances enthusiasm with cold, hard pragmatism. If you're serious about taking your side gig to the next level, it's time to buckle up and prepare for the ride of your life.

Step 1: Time Management

When you're juggling a full-time job with a side hustle, time becomes your most valuable asset. It's easy to burn out if you don't manage it effectively. The key to scaling your side hustle lies in optimizing the limited hours you have each day.

Start by assessing your current schedule. Identify time-wasting activities and eliminate them. This could mean cutting down on TV, minimizing social media scrolling, or even saying 'no' to non-essential social events. Use productivity tools like Trello or Asana to organize your tasks and keep track of deadlines.

One of the most successful strategies I've seen is batching tasks. Group similar tasks together—like content creation, customer communication, or administrative work—and dedicate specific blocks of time to them. This reduces the mental load of switching between tasks and increases efficiency.

Step 2: Reinvesting Profits.

One of the biggest mistakes new entrepreneurs make is pulling profits from their side hustle too soon. While it's tempting to start enjoying the fruits of your labor, reinvesting those early profits back into your business is crucial for sustainable growth.

Think of your side hustle like a sapling. It needs nurturing and resources to grow strong roots before it can flourish into a towering tree. Reinvesting profits could mean purchasing better tools, upgrading your website, investing in marketing, or even hiring help.

For example, if you're running an e-commerce store, consider reinvesting profits into inventory expansion, improving product photography, or running targeted ads. If you're a freelancer, you might want to invest in advanced training or software that can help you deliver higher quality work faster.

Step 3: Marketing on a Budget.

Marketing is the lifeblood of any growing business, but it doesn't have to drain your bank account. In fact, some of the most effective marketing strategies require little to no financial investment—just creativity and consistency.

Social media is a powerful tool that can help you reach a larger audience without spending a fortune. Focus on building a strong presence on platforms where your target audience hangs out. Whether it's Instagram, LinkedIn, TikTok, or YouTube, the key is to consistently provide value. Share your journey, offer tips, showcase your work, and engage with your audience.

Content marketing is another cost-effective strategy. Start a blog, create YouTube tutorials, or produce a podcast related to your niche. This not only positions you as an expert in your field but also drives organic traffic to your business.

Step 4: Financial and Legal Considerations.

As your side hustle grows, so do the financial and legal responsibilities. You have to lay a solid foundation to avoid pitfalls down the road.

1. Separate Finances: The first step is to separate your personal and business finances. Open a dedicated business bank account and get a business credit card. This makes it easier to track income and expenses, which is crucial come tax time.

2. Accounting and Taxes: Consider investing in accounting software like QuickBooks or hiring a part-time bookkeeper. Stay on top of your tax obligations—nothing can derail your growth faster than an unexpected tax bill. Research the tax deductions available to small business owners, such as home office expenses, business-related travel, and equipment costs.

3. Legal Structure: As your business grows, you'll need to consider its legal structure. Operating as a sole proprietor might be fine in the beginning, but as your revenue increases, it might make sense to form an LLC or a corporation. This not only provides legal protection but can also offer tax advantages.

4. Contracts: If you're providing services, always use contracts. A well-drafted contract protects both you and your clients, ensuring that everyone is on the same page regarding the scope of work, deadlines, and payment terms.

Step 5: Knowing When to Quit Your Day Job.

Perhaps the most significant decision you'll face as your side hustle grows is knowing when to quit your day job. It's a leap of faith that requires careful planning and consideration.

The first step is to ensure that your side hustle's income is consistent and sufficient to cover your living expenses. A good rule of thumb is to wait until your side hustle is generating at least 75-80% of your current salary. This ensures that you're not jumping ship too early and that your business can sustain itself.

Consider building an emergency fund that covers 6-12 months of living expenses. This provides a safety net should your business experience fluctuations in income.

Step 6: Scaling Up – From Hustle to Empire

Once you've made the transition, the real work begins. Scaling up your side hustle into a full-fledged business requires a different mindset and approach.

1. Delegation: As a one-person show, you've likely worn all the hats—marketing, sales, production, customer service. But as your business grows, delegation becomes essential. Identify areas where you can outsource tasks, whether it's hiring a virtual assistant, a marketing agency, or a production team. This frees up your time to focus on higher-level strategies and business growth.

2. Systems and Processes: Establishing efficient systems and processes is crucial for scalability. Document your workflows, automate repetitive tasks, and use project management tools to keep everything on track. The goal is to create a business that runs smoothly even when you're not there.

3. Continuous Learning: The entrepreneurial journey is one of continuous learning and adaptation. Stay informed about industry trends, invest in personal development, and never stop innovating. The most successful entrepreneurs are those who are always willing to learn and evolve.

4. Building a Brand: Finally, focus on building a strong brand. A well-defined brand differentiates you from competitors and creates a loyal customer base. Invest in professional branding, from your logo and website to your customer service and product packaging. Your brand is your business's identity—make it memorable.

Remember, every empire started as a simple idea. With passion, persistence, and a strategic approach, your side hustle can grow into something extraordinary. Embrace the journey, stay true to your values, and never lose sight of why you started in the first place.

CHAPTER 8

CRYPTO DECODED

UNDERSTANDING CRYPTOCURRENCY BASICS

"In the world of cryptocurrency, the only thing certain is uncertainty." – **Anonymous**

Cryptocurrency has become one of the most talked-about developments in finance and technology over the past decade. Whether you're curious about its potential to revolutionize money or skeptical of its volatile nature, there's no denying that digital currencies like Bitcoin have captured the world's imagination. As someone who has closely followed the rise of cryptocurrencies, I'm here to break down the basics, demystify the jargon, and provide a balanced view of this intriguing yet complex world.

It all started in 2008, during the global financial crisis when trust in traditional financial institutions was at an all-time low. In this context, a person (or group) using the pseudonym Satoshi Nakamoto published a whitepaper titled "Bitcoin: A Peer-to-Peer Electronic Cash System." This paper proposed a revolutionary idea: a decentralized form of currency that didn't rely on banks or governments to function.

By January 2009, the first Bitcoin was mined, marking the birth of cryptocurrency. Unlike the dollars in your wallet or the balance in your bank account, Bitcoin wasn't controlled by any central authority. Instead, it relied on a network of computers (known as nodes) that worked together to validate and record transactions. This was the dawn of a new era—one where money could exist purely in digital form, outside the control of traditional financial systems.

Blockchain: The Backbone of Cryptocurrency

To understand how Bitcoin and other cryptocurrencies work, you need to grasp the concept of blockchain technology. Think of a blockchain as a digital ledger—a record of transactions that is stored across a network of computers. But unlike a traditional ledger that might be kept by a bank, this one is decentralized, meaning that no single entity has control over it.

Here's a simple way to picture it: Imagine you and a group of friends are keeping track of who owes whom money. Instead of trusting one person to keep the record, you all decide to keep identical copies of the record on your phones. Every time a transaction is made, all of your records are updated simultaneously. This way, if someone tries to alter the record on their phone to cheat the system, the other copies will show the discrepancy, and the fraudulent transaction will be rejected.

That's essentially how blockchain works. Every time a transaction is made, it's bundled with others into a "block," which is then added to a "chain" of previous blocks. This chain of blocks, or blockchain, is what keeps the whole system secure and transparent. Each block contains a unique code (called a cryptographic hash) that links it to the previous block, making it virtually impossible to alter without changing every subsequent block—a task that would require enormous computational power.

Beyond Bitcoin

While Bitcoin was the first and remains the most well-known cryptocurrency, it's far from the only one. The success of Bitcoin inspired the creation of thousands of other digital currencies, each with its own unique features and use cases. Here's a brief overview of some of the major players in the cryptocurrency space:

1. Ethereum (ETH): Launched in 2015 by a young programmer named Vitalik Buterin, Ethereum is more than just a cryptocurrency—it's a decentralized platform that allows developers to build and deploy smart contracts and decentralized applications (dApps). While Bitcoin is often referred to as "digital gold," Ethereum is like the "world computer" that powers a new generation of blockchain-based applications.

2. Ripple (XRP): Unlike Bitcoin and Ethereum, which operate on public blockchains, Ripple is a digital payment protocol designed to facilitate fast and low-cost international money transfers. It's been adopted by several financial institutions as a way to streamline cross-border payments.

3. Litecoin (LTC): Often described as the "silver to Bitcoin's gold," Litecoin was created in 2011 by Charlie Lee, a former Google engineer. It's designed to be a faster and lighter version of Bitcoin, with a shorter block time (2.5 minutes compared to Bitcoin's 10 minutes) and a different hashing algorithm.

4. Cardano (ADA): Developed by a team of academics and engineers, Cardano aims to offer a more secure and scalable blockchain platform for smart contracts and dApps. It's often praised for its research-driven approach to development.

5. Binance Coin (BNB): Originally created as a utility token for the Binance cryptocurrency exchange, BNB has evolved into a multi-purpose cryptocurrency that can be used for transaction fees, payments, and even travel bookings.

These are just a few examples of the thousands of cryptocurrencies that exist today. Some are designed to serve as digital money, while others aim to revolutionize industries like finance, healthcare, and supply chain management.

Common Misconceptions About Cryptocurrency

Despite its growing popularity, cryptocurrency is still widely misunderstood. Let's clear up some of the most common misconceptions:

1. "Cryptocurrency is anonymous and untraceable."

While it's true that cryptocurrencies like Bitcoin offer a higher degree of privacy compared to traditional payment methods, they're not completely anonymous. Every transaction is recorded on the blockchain, which is a public ledger. While your name and address aren't tied to your Bitcoin wallet, your wallet's transaction history is visible to anyone who knows your wallet address. Law enforcement agencies have become increasingly adept at tracing cryptocurrency transactions back to individuals.

2. "Cryptocurrency is a get-rich-quick scheme."

Yes, some people have made fortunes by investing in cryptocurrencies, but many others have lost money. The market is notoriously volatile, with prices that can swing wildly in a matter of hours. Investing in cryptocurrency is highly speculative, and you just have to approach it with caution, only invest what you can afford to lose.

3. "Cryptocurrencies are just a fad."

While it's true that many cryptocurrencies have come and gone, the underlying technology—blockchain—is here to stay. Major financial institutions, corporations, and even governments are exploring ways to integrate blockchain into their operations. Whether or not individual cryptocurrencies survive, the technology behind them is likely to play a significant role in the future of finance and beyond.

4. "You need to buy a whole Bitcoin."

Given the high price of Bitcoin, many people think they can't afford to invest. But in reality, Bitcoin is divisible into smaller units, called satoshis (named after its mysterious creator, Satoshi Nakamoto). One Bitcoin equals 100 million satoshis, so you can buy a fraction of a Bitcoin that fits your budget.

Frequently Asked Questions About Cryptocurrency

As more people become interested in cryptocurrency, certain questions tend to come up repeatedly. Let me answer some of the most common ones:

1. "How do I buy cryptocurrency?"

Buying cryptocurrency is easier than ever, thanks to the proliferation of cryptocurrency exchanges like Coinbase, Binance, and Kraken. To get started, you'll need to create an account on an exchange, verify your identity, and link a payment method (like a bank account or credit card). Once you're set up, you can purchase a variety of cryptocurrencies with just a few clicks.

2. "Is cryptocurrency safe?"

Cryptocurrency transactions are secured by blockchain technology, which is incredibly difficult to hack. However, the exchanges where you buy and store your cryptocurrency can be vulnerable to hacking. It's essential to use strong passwords, enable two-factor authentication, and, if possible, store your cryptocurrency in a hardware wallet (a physical device that stores your private keys offline) to minimize the risk of theft.

3. "What can I do with cryptocurrency?"

While the primary use of cryptocurrency has been as an investment, there are growing ways to use it in everyday life. You can use Bitcoin and other cryptocurrencies to purchase goods and services, from buying a coffee at certain cafes to booking flights and hotels. Some people use cryptocurrency to transfer money internationally, taking advantage of lower fees and faster transactions compared to traditional banks.

4. "What are the risks of investing in cryptocurrency?"

The most significant risks include volatility, security breaches, and regulatory uncertainty. Cryptocurrency prices can fluctuate wildly, leading to significant gains or losses in a short period. Security breaches at exchanges have resulted in the theft of millions of dollars' worth of cryptocurrency. Additionally, the regulatory environment is still evolving, and future laws could impact the value or legality of certain cryptocurrencies.

5. "Is cryptocurrency legal?"

The legality of cryptocurrency varies by country. In most places, it's legal to buy, sell, and use cryptocurrency, but some countries have imposed restrictions or outright bans. It's crucial to understand the laws in your jurisdiction before engaging in cryptocurrency transactions.

The Future of Cryptocurrency: Excitement and Caution

Cryptocurrency represents a radical shift in how we think about money, ownership, and trust. It has the potential to democratize finance, offering people around the world access to a system that is decentralized, transparent, and borderless. However, this potential comes with risks. The technology is still in its early stages, and the market is rife with speculation, scams, and uncertainty.

For every story of someone who made a fortune with Bitcoin, there's another of someone who lost their savings in a market crash. The key is to approach cryptocurrency with a mix of excitement and caution. Educate yourself, start small, and never invest more than you can afford to lose.

As we look to the future, it's clear that cryptocurrency and blockchain technology are here to stay. Whether they will replace traditional financial systems or simply coexist with them remains to be seen. What's certain is that we're on the cusp of a new era—one where money, in its digital form, could transform the way we live, work, and interact with each other.

TO HODL OR NOT TO HODL: SMART STRATEGIES FOR CRYPTO INVESTING

"The stock market is filled with individuals who know the price of everything, but the value of nothing." — **Philip Fisher**

In the world of cryptocurrency, this quote resonates profoundly. Cryptocurrencies, with their allure of rapid gains and revolutionary potential, have attracted millions of investors worldwide. But as with any investment, particularly one as volatile as crypto, it's crucial to approach it with both excitement for the possibilities and a firm grasp of financial responsibility. Whether you're contemplating your first Bitcoin purchase or deciding whether to HODL (hold on for dear life) through the market's turbulent swings, having a clear strategy is essential.

Unlike traditional assets such as stocks or bonds, cryptocurrencies represent ownership in decentralized networks rather than companies or physical commodities. Bitcoin, for instance, is often seen as "digital gold," a store of value independent of any government or financial institution. Ethereum, on the other hand, is a platform for decentralized applications, with its cryptocurrency, Ether (ETH), serving as fuel for these applications.

But it's not just Bitcoin and Ethereum. There are thousands of cryptocurrencies, each with its own purpose, technology, and level of risk. Some aim to improve upon Bitcoin's design, while others focus on specific industries like finance, gaming, or data storage.

Strategy 1: Portfolio Allocation.

One of the cardinal rules of investing applies equally to crypto: don't put all your eggs in one basket. Diversification can help spread risk across different assets, reducing the impact of any single investment's poor performance on your overall portfolio.

When it comes to crypto, this means not just investing in multiple cryptocurrencies but also considering how much of your overall investment portfolio should be in crypto in the first place. While some enthusiasts might advocate for a heavy allocation, financial prudence suggests starting with a modest percentage—perhaps 1-

5% of your total portfolio—especially if you're new to the market.

Strategy 2: Risk Management.

Cryptocurrency markets are notoriously volatile. Prices can soar or plummet within hours, driven by factors ranging from regulatory news to tweets by influential figures. This volatility can be both exhilarating and terrifying, making risk management a crucial part of any crypto investment strategy.

One effective way to manage risk is through dollar-cost averaging (DCA). This strategy involves investing a fixed amount of money into cryptocurrency at regular intervals, regardless of the price. Over time, this can reduce the impact of short-term price fluctuations and prevent the emotional pitfalls of trying to time the market.

Another risk management strategy is setting stop-loss orders. These are pre-set instructions to sell a cryptocurrency if its price falls to a certain level. Stop-loss orders can protect against significant losses by automatically liquidating your position if the market moves against you. However, they're not foolproof—extreme volatility can lead to "flash crashes," where prices briefly dip before recovering, potentially triggering your stop-loss order unnecessarily.

Strategy 3: Long-Term vs. Short-Term Approaches.

Your investment horizon—how long you plan to hold your crypto assets—should align with your overall financial goals. Are you in it for quick gains, or do you believe in the long-term potential of blockchain technology?

HODLing: The term "HODL" originated from a typo in a Bitcoin forum and has since become a rallying cry for long-term crypto investors. HODLing involves holding onto your crypto assets through market ups and downs, betting that their value will increase over the long term. This approach requires patience and a strong belief in the future of cryptocurrency.

Trading: On the flip side, some investors prefer to take advantage of short-term price movements through trading. This approach requires a deep understanding of market trends, technical analysis, and a willingness to spend time monitoring the market. While trading can yield significant profits, it's also riskier and can lead to substantial losses if the market moves against you.

Strategy 4: Exploring Different Investment Methods

There's more than one way to invest in cryptocurrency. Each method has its own set of pros and cons, depending on your goals, risk tolerance, and level of expertise.

Direct Purchase: The most straightforward way to invest in cryptocurrency is by buying it directly on an exchange like Coinbase, Binance, or Kraken. This method gives you full control over your assets, allowing you to store them in a digital wallet and use them as you see fit. However, direct purchase also requires you to manage your own security, including safeguarding your private keys and protecting against hacks.

Cryptocurrency ETFs: For those who prefer a more traditional investment vehicle, cryptocurrency exchange-traded funds (ETFs) offer exposure to crypto without the need to buy and store the assets directly. ETFs like the Bitcoin Strategy ETF (BITO) invest in Bitcoin futures contracts rather than Bitcoin itself, offering a way to gain exposure to the crypto market within a regulated framework. However, ETFs can come with management fees and may not fully capture the upside of owning cryptocurrency directly.

Mining: Cryptocurrency mining involves using computing power to solve complex mathematical problems, thereby validating transactions on the blockchain and earning rewards in the form of new cryptocurrency. While mining can be profitable, it's also resource-intensive, requiring significant investment in hardware, electricity, and technical know-how. As cryptocurrencies like Bitcoin become more established, mining difficulty increases, making it harder for individual miners to compete with large mining operations.

Staking: Some cryptocurrencies, like Ethereum (following its transition to proof-of-stake) and Cardano, allow you to "stake" your coins to help secure the network and validate transactions. In return, you earn rewards in the form of additional cryptocurrency. Staking offers a way to generate passive income from your crypto holdings, but it also comes with risks, such as the potential loss of staked assets if the network is compromised.

DeFi (Decentralized Finance): DeFi platforms offer a wide range of financial services, from lending and borrowing to yield farming and liquidity provision, all without the need for traditional intermediaries like banks. By participating in DeFi, you can earn interest on your crypto assets or provide liquidity to decentralized exchanges in exchange for rewards. However, DeFi is still a relatively new and experimental field, with significant risks related to smart contract vulnerabilities, platform hacks, and regulatory uncertainty.

Successes and Failures

Crypto investing can lead to both spectacular successes and crushing failures. Understanding the experiences of others can provide valuable insights into the risks and rewards of this volatile market.

Success Story: In 2011, Kristoffer Koch, a Norwegian engineer, bought $27 worth of Bitcoin while researching encryption. He quickly forgot about his investment until 2013, when he rediscovered it. By then, his initial $27 investment had grown to be worth over $800,000. Koch's story illustrates the power of early investment and long-term holding in the crypto market.

Failure Story: On the flip side, we have the cautionary tale of a Reddit user who, in 2018, mortgaged his house to buy Bitcoin at its all-time high, just before the market crashed. Over the next year, Bitcoin's value plummeted by more than 80%, leaving the investor with significant losses and a mortgage to repay. This story serves as a reminder of the dangers of investing more than you can afford to lose and the importance of timing in such a volatile market.

Cryptocurrency presents a unique blend of opportunities and risks. The potential for rapid gains, the thrill of participating in a technological revolution, and the allure of decentralized finance are undeniably exciting. However, these opportunities come with significant volatility, regulatory uncertainty, and the risk of substantial financial loss.

As you consider your crypto investment strategy, remember that there's no one-size-fits-all approach. Whether you choose to HODL, trade, or explore other investment methods, it's crucial to stay informed, manage your risks, and align your strategy with your financial goals and risk tolerance. Crypto investing is about making smart, informed decisions that can help you build wealth over time while protecting your financial future.

CHAPTER 9

THE RETIREMENT RIDDLE

401(K)S, IRAS, AND WTFS

"The best time to start thinking about your retirement is before the boss does." — **Anonymous**

Retirement planning can feel like a murky, jargon-filled world, but the truth is, it's just like ordering drinks at a bar. You've got your classics, your trendy options, and that one weird concoction your friend swears by but you're pretty sure is just a terrible idea. The key is knowing what you're ordering, how it fits your taste, and what it'll cost you in the long run.

So, let's pull up a stool, grab a pint, and break down the retirement options available to you, from the trusty 401(k) to the Roth IRA. By the end of this, you'll know the difference between a tax deduction and a tax deferral, and you'll be able to make informed decisions that'll keep you sipping mojitos on the beach well into your golden years.

401(k): The Classic Choice, Served with a Side of Employer Matching

First up is the 401(k), the old reliable of retirement accounts. Think of it as the craft beer your local brewery has been perfecting for years. It's solid, dependable, and if your employer offers a match, it comes with a free side of nachos.

A 401(k) is an employer-sponsored retirement account where you can contribute a portion of your pre-tax salary. The money you contribute grows tax-deferred, meaning you don't pay taxes on it until you withdraw it in retirement. The best part? Many employers offer a match—essentially free money they contribute to your account based on what you put in. It's like a buy-one-get-one-free deal on your favorite beer. If your employer offers a match, take full advantage. Contribute at least enough to get the full match because turning down free money is like refusing that second beer—it just doesn't make sense.

Contribution Limits: As of 2024, you can contribute up to $22,500 per year to your 401(k). If you're over 50, you get a little something extra—an additional $7,500 in catch-up contributions, because who doesn't love a bonus round?

Tax Implications: Contributions are made with pre-tax dollars, which lowers your taxable income for the year. However, when you start withdrawing money in retirement, those withdrawals will be taxed as regular income. This is where you'll want to consider your future tax bracket—will you be paying more or less in taxes when you retire?

Employer Matching: The exact matching formula varies by employer, but a common setup is a 50% match on contributions up to 6% of your salary. So, if you make $60,000 a year and contribute 6% ($3,600), your employer might chip in an additional $1,800.

Vesting: Keep in mind that employer contributions may be subject to a vesting schedule, meaning you need to stay with the company for a certain number of years before you can take their contributions with you if you leave. It's like having to wait a few rounds before you can grab that free drink your buddy promised.

Traditional IRA: The Flexible Option with a Tax Break Today

Next, we've got the Traditional IRA (Individual Retirement Account). This one's like a classic cocktail—simple, effective, and perfect for any occasion. Whether you're employed, self-employed, or unemployed, you can open a Traditional IRA, making it one of the most flexible retirement options out there.

Contribution Limits: In 2024, you can contribute up to $6,500 annually, or $7,500 if you're over 50. This limit applies to the combined total you can contribute to both a Traditional and Roth IRA.

Tax Implications: Contributions to a Traditional IRA are typically tax-deductible, meaning they reduce your taxable income for the year. However, like the 401(k), your money grows tax-deferred, and withdrawals in retirement are taxed as ordinary income. This makes a Traditional IRA a great option if you want a tax break now and believe you'll be in a lower tax bracket when you retire.

Eligibility: If you or your spouse have a retirement plan at work, your ability to deduct your IRA contributions may be limited based on your income. This is like the bartender cutting you off after one too many—don't say we didn't warn you.

Roth IRA: The Hipster's Choice, with Future Tax-Free Withdrawals

Now let's talk about the Roth IRA, the trendy, Instagrammable cocktail of retirement accounts. Unlike the Traditional IRA, a Roth IRA is funded with after-tax dollars, meaning you don't get a tax break today, but your future self will thank you. Why? Because all qualified withdrawals in retirement are completely tax-free.

Contribution Limits: The contribution limits for a Roth IRA are the same as for a Traditional IRA—$6,500 annually, or $7,500 if you're over 50.

Tax Implications: The beauty of the Roth IRA is in its tax treatment. Since you've already paid taxes on the money you contribute, you won't owe any taxes on your withdrawals in retirement. This can be especially beneficial if you expect to be in a higher tax bracket later on or if tax rates increase in the future. Imagine retiring and enjoying your hard-earned money without Uncle Sam taking another sip.

Eligibility: Roth IRAs do have income limits for eligibility. In 2024, if you're single and your modified adjusted gross income (MAGI) is $153,000 or more, your ability to contribute to a Roth IRA begins to phase out. For married couples filing jointly, this limit starts at $228,000. So, if you're making the big bucks, you might be out of luck, but there are backdoor strategies (like a Roth conversion) to get around these limits if you're feeling crafty.

SEP IRA and SIMPLE IRA: The Entrepreneur's Special

For the self-employed and small business owners out there, SEP (Simplified Employee Pension) IRAs and SIMPLE (Savings Incentive Match Plan for Employees) IRAs are like those craft beers that only a few bars carry—they're designed for a specific crowd, but they're oh-so-good if you know what you're looking for.

SEP IRA: This is an excellent option if you're self-employed or run a small business. With a SEP IRA, you can contribute up to 25% of your net earnings from self-employment, up to a whopping $66,000 in 2024. Contributions are tax-deductible, and the money grows tax-deferred until retirement. The simplicity and high contribution limits make this an attractive choice if you've got fluctuating income or want to maximize your retirement savings in good years.

SIMPLE IRA: The SIMPLE IRA is designed for small businesses with 100 or fewer employees. It's a bit like a 401(k) but with less administrative hassle and lower contribution limits. Employees can contribute up to $15,500 in 2024, with an additional $3,500 catch-up contribution if you're over 50. Employers are required to either match contributions up to 3% of the employee's salary or contribute 2% of the employee's salary, whether the employee contributes or not. It's simple, as the name suggests, and effective for businesses that want to offer a retirement plan without the complexity of a 401(k).

Other Retirement Vehicles: The Quirky Options

Let's not forget some of the more niche options out there. These are like the quirky, one-off cocktails that only a few know about but can be the perfect fit for the right person.

HSA (Health Savings Account): While not strictly a retirement account, an HSA can be a powerful retirement tool. Contributions are tax-deductible, grow tax-free, and can be withdrawn tax-free for qualified medical expenses. After age 65, you can withdraw HSA funds for any reason without penalty, though you'll pay taxes on non-medical withdrawals. It's like getting a tax-free drink today and another tax-free drink tomorrow.

403(b) and 457(b) Plans: These are similar to 401(k)s but are available to employees of public schools, non-profits, and government organizations. Contribution limits are the same as for 401(k)s, and the tax treatment is identical. If you work in the public sector, these plans are worth considering, especially since some 457(b) plans allow penalty-free withdrawals before age 59½.

Solo 401(k): This is a 401(k) designed specifically for self-employed individuals with no employees (except maybe a spouse). The contribution limits are the same as a traditional 401(k), but you can contribute both as an employer and an employee, potentially allowing for more substantial savings than with a SEP IRA.

The Bottom Line: Choose Your Poison Wisely

Retirement planning might not be as fun as a night out with friends, but it's one of the most important financial decisions you'll ever make. Each of these retirement accounts offers unique benefits, and the right one for you depends on your situation, your goals, and your future tax outlook. The key is to start early, contribute consistently, and adjust your strategy as your life and financial situation evolve.

The Fire Movement: Is Early Retirement Possible?

"You can't get much done in life if you only work on the days when you feel good." — **Jerry West**

Early retirement—sounds like a dream, right? Imagine waking up on a Monday morning without the jarring alarm, sipping coffee while the world rushes to their nine-to-fives, knowing you've achieved what so many others only fantasize about. This dream is the cornerstone of the FIRE movement—Financial Independence, Retire Early—a lifestyle that has captured the imagination of many, especially millennials and Gen Zers. But is it truly possible, or is it just another internet-fueled fantasy?

What Is FIRE?

At its core, the FIRE movement is about achieving financial independence as quickly as possible so you can retire early—sometimes decades earlier than the traditional retirement age. Financial independence, in this context, means having enough money saved and invested that your passive income (from investments, side gigs, or other sources) covers your living expenses indefinitely.

The FIRE movement revolves around three key principles:

1. **Aggressive Saving and Investing**: This is the backbone of FIRE. Proponents often save 50-70% of their income, far more than the standard 10-15% financial advisors typically recommend. The goal is to amass a substantial nest egg as quickly as possible.

2. **Frugality**: Cutting costs and living below your means is another pillar of FIRE. The less you need to live comfortably, the sooner you can retire. This often involves sacrifices like downsizing your home, driving an older car, or skipping out on luxuries.

3. **Investing for Growth**: Rather than letting your money sit in a savings account, FIRE followers invest in assets that have the potential for growth, such as stocks, real estate, or index funds. The idea is to maximize the return on your investments to reach financial independence faster.

Different Approaches to FIRE

Not all FIRE enthusiasts are created equal. Depending on your lifestyle goals and financial situation, there are different flavors of FIRE, each with its unique approach and philosophy:

1. **Lean FIRE**: This is the bare-bones version of FIRE. If you're pursuing Lean FIRE, you're focused on retiring as soon as possible with a minimalistic lifestyle. This might mean living in a tiny house, embracing extreme frugality, or moving to a low-cost-of-living area. Lean FIRE followers often aim to live on $40,000 or less per year.

2. **Fat FIRE**: On the other end of the spectrum, Fat FIRE is about retiring early without sacrificing a comfortable lifestyle. Fat FIRE adherents aim for a higher level of financial independence, typically saving enough to fund a more luxurious retirement with annual expenses of $100,000 or more. This approach requires a larger nest egg but allows for more freedom and indulgence in retirement.

3. **Barista FIRE**: A middle ground between Lean and Fat FIRE, Barista FIRE is a strategy where you achieve partial financial independence and then take on a part-time job (often with benefits like health insurance) to cover the gap. It's a way to retire from a high-stress career but still keep some income flowing to support a modest lifestyle.

4. **Coast FIRE**: This approach is all about building your retirement savings early and then letting compound interest do the heavy lifting. With Coast FIRE, you save aggressively in your 20s and 30s and then reduce your savings rate in your 40s and 50s, allowing your investments to grow on their own until you're ready to retire.

The Appeal of FIRE

The allure of FIRE is undeniable. The promise of escaping the rat race, living life on your terms, and spending your days doing what you love is enough to make anyone dream. For many, the idea of financial independence isn't just about money—it's about freedom. Freedom from the daily grind, from office politics, from the stress of living paycheck to paycheck.

Some of the key benefits that attract people to the FIRE movement includes:

1. **Freedom to Pursue Passions**: Without the need to work for a living, you're free to spend your time on hobbies, creative pursuits, or volunteer work. Imagine finally writing that novel, starting a nonprofit, or traveling the world—these dreams become realities with FIRE.

2. **Improved Mental Health**: The stress of modern work can take a toll on mental health. By retiring early, many FIRE followers report feeling less anxious and more in control of their lives. The ability to step away from the pressure of a demanding job can lead to greater happiness and well-being.

3. **More Time with Loved Ones**: FIRE allows you to spend more time with family and friends. Whether it's raising your children, caring for aging parents, or simply enjoying more quality time with your spouse, early retirement can strengthen your relationships.

4. **Control Over Your Life**: FIRE gives you the power to say no—to jobs you don't want, to bosses you don't like, to lifestyles that don't suit you. It's about reclaiming control over how you spend your days and who you spend them with.

The Realities and Challenges of FIRE

While the FIRE movement offers an enticing vision of the future, it's not without its challenges. The road to financial independence is paved with sacrifices, hard work, and a fair share of risk. Here are some of the realities you'll need to consider if you're thinking about joining the FIRE movement:

1. **Extreme Frugality Isn't for Everyone**: Cutting back on expenses to save 50-70% of your income requires a level of discipline and sacrifice that not everyone is willing to make. It can mean living in a smaller home, forgoing vacations, and saying no to social events that cost money. For some, this level of frugality can feel like a burden rather than a pathway to freedom.

2. **The Risk of Outliving Your Savings**: One of the biggest fears for those pursuing FIRE is the possibility of outliving their savings. With people living longer than ever, there's a real risk that your nest egg might not last as long as you do. This is especially true if you retire in your 30s or 40s and have 50+ years of expenses to cover.

3. **Market Volatility**: FIRE followers often rely heavily on investments in the stock market to grow their savings. However, the market is unpredictable, and a significant downturn could jeopardize your financial independence. It's essential to have a diversified portfolio and a contingency plan in case things don't go as expected.

4. **Healthcare Costs**: For many early retirees, healthcare is a significant concern. Without

employer-sponsored health insurance, you'll need to find a way to cover healthcare costs, which can be substantial. Options like the Affordable Care Act or Health Savings Accounts (HSAs) can help, but it's a challenge that requires careful planning.

5. **Social Isolation**: Retiring early can sometimes lead to feelings of isolation, especially if your friends and peers are still working. It's important to find a community of like-minded individuals or activities that keep you engaged and connected.

6. **Purpose and Identity**: Work often provides a sense of purpose and identity. For some, leaving the workforce can lead to feelings of aimlessness or a loss of identity. It's crucial to have a plan for how you'll spend your time and find fulfillment in early retirement.

Is FIRE Right for You?

The FIRE movement isn't a one-size-fits-all solution. It requires careful planning, disciplined saving, and a willingness to embrace a lifestyle that might differ significantly from the norm. If you're someone who values freedom and is willing to make sacrifices to achieve it, FIRE could be an appealing path.

However, it's also important to approach FIRE with a healthy dose of realism. The journey to financial independence is long and challenging, and it's not without its risks. Before diving in, consider your own financial situation, your willingness to live frugally, and your appetite for risk.

Ultimately, the decision to pursue FIRE is a deeply personal one. It's about weighing the appeal of early retirement against the sacrifices required to get there. For some, the promise of freedom and control over their lives is worth the effort. For others, a more traditional approach to retirement might be a better fit.

In the end, the question isn't just whether early retirement is possible—it's whether it's the right choice for you. Whether you're planning to retire at 40 or 65, the most important thing is to have a plan that aligns with your goals, values, and lifestyle.

CHAPTER 10

LIVING RICH

THE ART OF MINDFUL SPENDING

"The price of anything is the amount of life you exchange for it." — **Henry David Thoreau**

In a world that constantly pulls us in the direction of more—more stuff, more experiences, more spending—finding a balance between enjoying life's pleasures and maintaining financial health can feel like walking a tightrope. You want to savor that gourmet dinner, take that spontaneous weekend trip, or buy that new gadget. Yet, there's often a nagging guilt that creeps in, whispering that every dollar spent is a dollar lost from your future.

But what if I told you there's a way to indulge in life's joys without the guilt? As a financial coach, I believe in the power of balanced living—a philosophy that allows you to enjoy the present without sacrificing your future. The key lies in mindful spending, a practice rooted in value-based decisions that align your financial choices with what truly brings you joy and fulfillment.

Understanding Value-Based Spending

At the heart of mindful spending is the concept of value-based spending. This approach encourages you to spend money on things that genuinely enhance your life and align with your personal values, while cutting back on expenses that don't contribute to your happiness.

Value-based spending begins with introspection. Ask yourself, what do you truly value? Is it spending time with loved ones? Traveling the world? Indulging in fine dining? Or perhaps it's investing in your education or health. Understanding what brings you the most satisfaction is the first step in making spending decisions that are not only guilt-free but also deeply fulfilling.

Identifying What Brings True Joy

Once you've identified your core values, the next step is to differentiate between true joy and fleeting pleasure. It's easy to get caught up in the thrill of instant gratification—a new outfit, a fancy dinner, or the latest tech gadget. But not all pleasures are created equal. True joy is sustainable, enriching your life in a meaningful way long after the initial thrill has faded.

To identify what brings true joy, reflect on past experiences. What purchases or activities have left you feeling genuinely content and fulfilled? What moments brought you lasting happiness? Perhaps it was a family vacation, a quiet evening spent reading, or a dinner party with close friends. On the other hand, think about the times when you spent money impulsively. How did you feel afterward? Did the purchase bring lasting joy, or was it followed by regret or indifference?

By becoming more aware of what truly enhances your life, you can make more intentional spending choices that align with your values and bring genuine satisfaction.

Strategies for Guilt-Free Indulgence

Now that you have a clearer understanding of your values and what brings you joy, let's talk about how to indulge in life's pleasures without the guilt.

1. **Plan for "Fun Money" in Your Budget**: One of the best ways to enjoy indulgences without guilt is to plan for them. Create a budget that includes a specific category for "fun money"—an amount you can spend on non-essential pleasures each month. Knowing that you've set aside money for enjoyment allows you to indulge guilt-free, as these expenses are already accounted for in your financial plan.

2. **Prioritize Your Indulgences**: Since resources are limited, it's important to prioritize your indulgences. Focus on spending money on experiences or items that align most closely with your values and bring

you the greatest joy. For example, if travel is a top priority, you might choose to allocate more of your fun money to vacations and cut back on dining out. By prioritizing, you can indulge in what matters most to you without overextending your budget.

3. **Embrace the Concept of "Enough"**: Our consumer-driven society often pushes the idea that more is better. But the truth is, there's a point where more doesn't add to your happiness—it just adds to your expenses. Embrace the concept of "enough" by recognizing when you've reached a level of satisfaction that doesn't require further spending. This mindset shift can help you avoid unnecessary purchases and focus on what truly matters.

4. **Make Indulgences Special**: One way to enhance the joy of indulgence is to make it a special occasion. Rather than indulging in small pleasures frequently, save them for when they'll have the most impact. For example, instead of buying your favorite treat every day, save it for the end of the week as a reward. This not only makes the experience more enjoyable but also helps you appreciate it more fully.

    1. **Practice Gratitude**: Gratitude is a powerful tool for enhancing happiness and reducing the desire

for more. By focusing on what you already have and appreciating the small joys in life, you can reduce the impulse to spend money on things that don't bring lasting fulfillment. Take time each day to reflect on the things you're grateful for—whether it's a beautiful sunset, a good book, or a meaningful conversation. This practice can help shift your mindset from one of scarcity to one of abundance.

Balancing Enjoyment with Financial Goals

While indulging in life's pleasures is important, it's equally crucial to stay on track with your financial goals. The key to balancing enjoyment with financial responsibility lies in mindful planning and consistent reflection.

Start by setting clear financial goals, whether it's paying off debt, building an emergency fund, saving for a down payment, or planning for retirement. Once you've established these goals, create a budget that allocates a portion of your income toward them. This ensures that you're making progress toward your financial future while still allowing room for enjoyment in the present.

Regularly review your spending to ensure it aligns with your values and goals. If you find that certain expenses aren't bringing you the joy you expected, consider redirecting those funds toward something that will. Remember, mindful spending isn't about deprivation—it's about making intentional choices that enhance your life both now and in the future.

ALIGNING YOUR FINANCES WITH YOUR VALUES

"Too many people spend money they haven't earned, to buy things they don't want, to impress people they don't like." — **Will Rogers**

Money is more than just numbers in a bank account or the means to buy things. It's a reflection of our choices, priorities, and, ultimately, our values. In a world that often equates financial success with net worth, it's easy to lose sight of what truly matters. But what if we flipped the script? What if, instead of letting our money dictate our lives, we used it as a tool to build a life that resonates with our deepest values?

This journey of aligning your finances with your values isn't about following a prescribed path to wealth. It's about introspection, intentionality, and redefining success on your own terms.

Defining Success Beyond Net Worth

Before diving into the nuts and bolts of value-based financial planning, it's crucial to take a step back and ask yourself: *What does success look like for me?* Society often measures success by how much money you make, the car you drive, or the size of your home. But these are external metrics, shaped by societal expectations rather than personal fulfillment.

True success is deeply personal. It's about living a life that aligns with your values and brings you genuine satisfaction. For some, this might mean having the freedom to travel, spending quality time with family, or making a positive impact on the community. For others, it might involve pursuing creative passions, achieving personal growth, or building meaningful relationships.

Take a moment to reflect on your life. What are the moments that have brought you the most joy and fulfillment? What are the experiences you cherish most? These are the moments that define success—not the numbers in your bank account.

Aligning Money Management with Your Values

Once you've defined what success means to you, the next step is to align your financial decisions with those values. This means making choices that not only support your financial well-being but also resonate with your principles and life goals.

1. Ethical Investing: Putting Your Money Where Your Beliefs Are

Investing is one of the most powerful ways to grow your wealth, but it's also an opportunity to support causes you believe in. Ethical investing, also known as socially responsible investing (SRI), allows you to put your money into companies and industries that align with your values.

Ethical investing isn't just about avoiding companies that engage in harmful practices; it's about actively choosing to invest in those that make a positive impact. For example, you might invest in companies that prioritize environmental sustainability, fair labor practices, or social justice initiatives.

When considering ethical investments, ask yourself: What do I want my money to support? What kind of world do I want to help create? By aligning your investments with your values, you can grow your wealth while contributing to causes that matter to you.

2. Charitable Giving: Using Wealth to Make a Difference

One of the most direct ways to align your finances with your values is through charitable giving. Whether it's donating to a local charity, supporting a global cause, or funding educational opportunities, charitable giving allows you to use your resources to make a positive impact on the world.

Consider what causes resonate with you the most. Is it education, healthcare, environmental conservation, or social justice? Once you've identified your priorities, you can create a giving strategy that reflects your values.

Charitable giving is a way to connect with your community, support those in need, and leave a legacy that goes beyond material wealth.

3. Career Choices: Pursuing Fulfillment Over Salary

In our careers, it's easy to get caught up in the pursuit of higher salaries, promotions, and job titles. While financial security is important, it's equally important to consider whether your career aligns with your values and brings you fulfillment.

Think about your current job. Does it align with your passions and values? Does it give you a sense of purpose, or is it simply a means to a paycheck? If your work feels disconnected from your values, it might be time to reassess your career path.

Pursuing a career that aligns with your values might mean making sacrifices in the short term—perhaps accepting a lower salary or taking on a less prestigious role. But in the long term, the fulfillment and satisfaction you gain from doing work that matters to you will far outweigh the financial trade-offs.

Consider what drives you—whether it's helping others, creating something new, or solving complex problems. Seek out opportunities that allow you to align your career with these passions. Remember, success is all about doing work that you find meaningful and fulfilling.

Creating a Value-Based Financial Plan

Aligning your finances with your values requires more than just making ethical choices—it requires a comprehensive financial plan that supports your life goals.

1. Set Financial Goals That Reflect Your Values

Start by setting financial goals that align with your values and definition of success. For example, if you value financial independence, your goal might be to build a robust emergency fund or invest in assets that generate passive income. If giving back is important to you, you might set a goal to donate a certain percentage of your income to charity each year.

When setting goals, make sure they are specific, measurable, achievable, relevant, and time-bound (SMART). This will help you stay focused and motivated as you work toward aligning your finances with your values.

2. Budget with Intention

A budget is a powerful tool for managing your finances, but it's also an opportunity to align your spending with your values. Start by categorizing your expenses based on your values. For example, if health and wellness are important to you, allocate a portion of your budget to nutritious food, gym memberships, or mental health services.

When creating your budget, prioritize spending on things that bring you joy and fulfillment. At the same time, look for areas where you can cut back on expenses that don't align with your values. By budgeting with intention, you can ensure that your money is being used in a way that supports your goals and principles.

As your life evolves, your values and priorities may shift, and your financial plan should adapt accordingly. Don't be afraid to make changes if something no longer feels right. The key is to remain flexible and open to reassessing your financial choices as needed.

Conclusion

As you close this book, remember that the journey toward financial literacy, fulfillment, and success is uniquely yours. You've gained insights, strategies, and a new perspective on how to align your money with your values, and now it's time to put that knowledge into action. Every small step you take towards mindful spending, ethical investing, or planning for your future is a step toward living the life you truly want.

But this journey doesn't have to end here. If this book has inspired or helped you in any way, I'd be deeply grateful if you shared your thoughts by leaving a positive review and rating on Amazon. Your feedback not only helps other readers discover the value within these pages, but it also encourages me to continue sharing ideas that can empower and uplift.

Thank you for taking this journey with me—may your path be filled with purpose, prosperity, and profound joy.